State Colleges
and Universities

THE LIBRARY OF EDUCATION

A Project of The Center for Applied Research in Education, Inc.

G. R. Gottschalk, Director

Categories of Coverage

I	II	III
Curriculum and Teaching	Administration, Organization, and Finance	Psychology

IV	V	VI
History, Philosophy, and Social Foundations	Professional Skills	Educational Institutions

State Colleges
and Universities

JOHN T. WAHLQUIST

President
San Jose State College

JAMES W. THORNTON, JR.

Professor of Education
San Jose State College

The Center for Applied Research in Education, Inc.
Washington, D.C.

370
L61
47095

June 1964

PRINTED IN THE UNITED STATES OF AMERICA

Foreword

Higher education is rapidly becoming one of the nation's largest enterprises. Capital investment in plant and equipment of American colleges and universities increased from slightly more than 8.9 billion dollars in 1956 to almost 13.6 billion in 1959. During the same period the current budget for operating expenses, auxiliary services, and student aid increased from 3.5 to 5.6 billion. In 1962 there were 3,614,344 degree-credit students enrolled in the nation's four-year institutions of higher education and of these well over two million were in public four-year colleges and universities. Furthermore, it is certain that these impressive figures will soon be dwarfed by those to follow. Estimates of collegiate enrollments for the future vary from a conservative doubling to a liberal tripling within approximately ten years.

Despite the anticipated growth of junior colleges, it will be the state-controlled four-year institutions which will accommodate the bulk of the enrollment increase. These institutions face grave responsibilities as they are called upon to serve unprecedented numbers of students in a society that demands quality along with quantity and that also increasingly demands efficiency and economy in operation. Such a context gives rise to a host of interrelated problems. These include the possible differentiation of functions among institutions, selection of students, coordination of and cooperation among colleges, and financial support for the college enterprise.

It need hardly be said that most Americans have a stake in their public colleges and universities and thus need to understand them and their problems to the fullest extent. Certainly this is true for potential students and their parents as well as for those in other educational institutions who prepare students to attend four-year institutions. But it is equally important that the general public become knowledgeable about the institutions which it supports and from which will stem much of the talent to advance the general welfare of society.

The authors of this volume have dealt succinctly and well with the subject of the country's state colleges and universities. Their treatment is comprehensive and clear. The reader will find it possible to place these types of institutions within the context of higher education generally and to observe trends in curriculum, relationships of colleges and the federal government, methods of state coordination, and crucial problems faced by state institutions.

Public higher education is not only big business, but it is also everybody's business. This volume serves well as a report on the enterprise.

LELAND L. MEDSKER

Vice-Chairman
Center for the Study of Higher Education
University of California

State Colleges and Universities

by John T. Wahlquist
and James W. Thornton, Jr.

The volume on *State Colleges and Universities* by Wahlquist and Thornton is closely related to certain other books in the Library of Education series, each of which treats a specialized kind of institution of higher education in the United States. The volumes of this nature already published are: *The Municipal University* by William S. Carlson; *The Smaller Liberal Arts College,* by Lewis B. Mayhew; and *The Church-Related College,* by Myron F. Wicke. The Wahlquist and Thornton book, like the one by Carlson, treats a sharply defined category of colleges and universities. In the Appendix the authors list some 380 state-controlled institutions of higher education, grouped into ten classifications; date of founding and fall term enrollment in 1961 are shown for each of the listed institutions.

The authors describe effectively the manner in which the state colleges and universities have evolved into their present status, and the forces that have led to these developments. The point of view expressed is that all institutions, in response to pressures from the demands for service in their constituent areas, tend to evolve toward the university-type organization and curriculum. In addition to the extensive treatment of the relation of the state colleges and universities to the state governments that sponsor and support them, an informative chapter is included on the relation of the federal government of the United States to the institutions of higher education.

JOHN DALE RUSSELL
Content Editor

Contents

CHAPTER I

State Higher Education in
the United States

American geography and American political and cultural history have led to the development of indigenous patterns of higher education. There is such diversity in fiscal controls, in educational purposes, and in standards of admission and performance that it is misleading to speak of a system of state higher education in the United States. The observer who is accustomed to unified national provisions for higher education may well find the American scene bewildering, amorphous, undisciplined, and dangerously heterogeneous. At the same time, native observers will find much to commend in the independence, the vitality, the adaptation to local needs, and the continuous capacity for change of American institutions of higher education. A brief description of some of the causes of this diversity will help to clarify the descriptions of the several broad categories of institutions.

The comparatively rapid settlement of America contributed to diversity of higher education, since colleges were often developed to afford opportunity for higher education to citizens of new states or territories. These colleges grew without frequent communication with other colleges; they were governed, as were the states and territories, by elected representatives of the people. They developed courses of study that seemed of most value to the people they served. One of the salient historical facts about American universities and colleges is that the definition of their role is transmitted from people to trustees to faculty to students, as compared to the much greater independence of faculty and students that characterizes higher education in other nations.

The idea that every man should have opportunity to develop his own capacities was another influence on American higher education. Social and economic mobility were closely associated with

1

informed intelligence and with highly schooled competence. Self-selection for higher education was seen as an essential element of democracy, and if one kind of institution did not seem to provide enough opportunity of the desired character at an available site, new institutions were freely established.

The sources of support and control contributed another dimension of diversification. The first (and still the most numerous class of institutions of higher education) were those *privately* established, by religious or other interests, and supported and controlled almost entirely without dependence on national, state, or local governments. Later, *publicly* supported and controlled colleges and universities were established by the federal government, states, municipalities, counties, and local districts. The majority of these public institutions—those established, controlled, and supported by the states—is the subject of this volume.

Because of recent growth in enrollments, the earlier distinctions between kinds of state institutions have lost some of their sharpness. It is still possible, however, to present a coherent description of significant developments in higher education by tracing the histories of the several varieties of state institutions.

Independent Institutions of Higher Education

The original colleges in colonial America were under private and sectarian control, even though their public value was recognized by the grant of public lands and public funds for their support. The association of religious bodies with collegiate foundations has been a strong and continuing tradition in the United States, although their dependence on some degree of public support began to wane during the first half of the eighteenth century and was practically discontinued from the ratification of the Constitution until the period after World War II. Of the 1313 private institutions listed in the *Education Directory 1959–60,* 793 are maintained under the control of churches; of the 520 nondenominational independent colleges, a high proportion were established by adherents of a church, but were later secularized as they grew in size and in scope of program and in fiscal independence. Of the total of 1313 private institutions, as many as 1205 emphasize liberal arts education, either in combination with one or more specialized curriculums or as the only offering.[1]

The importance of private higher education in American life is indicated numerically by comparison of the 1313 private colleges with the 12 federally controlled institutions, 375 state-controlled, and 311 under district or city control. In enrollments, the private colleges and universities accounted in 1960 for 40.8 per cent of total enrollments. If enrollments in the junior colleges and teachers' colleges are disregarded, private colleges enrolled 50.1 per cent of the remaining students.

The importance of the privately controlled college, however, transcends the purely quantitative. State-supported institutions are under constant pressure to emphasize the applied and practical aspects of research and instruction. The private colleges can counter-act some of this immediacy by concentrating—as their liberal arts nature implies—on purpose, order, and direction. In addition, the private colleges and universities safeguard for the nation the benefits of diversity and help to avoid the deadening effects of uniformity and intellectual inbreeding. They can emphasize, as public institutions may not, the values of religious dedication and understanding. With less criticism and less delay, they can experiment and innovate, and so provide a constant measuring stick for public institutions. Not the least of their values is their opportunity to intensify their pursuit of excellence through rigid selection of students and single-minded concentration on limited objectives. In these ways, the private colleges contribute essential values not readily attainable otherwise.

The State University

The state university is defined as "an institutional unit which offers programs leading to the doctor of philosophy or equivalent degree and has three or more professional schools as well as liberal arts and general programs, whether or not the word 'university' is found in its official name." A subtype of state university "also has the legal designation in its state of a 'land-grant college,' and receives funds from the Federal Government under the conditions of the

[1] U.S. Department of Health, Education, and Welfare, Office of Education, "Higher Education," in *Education Directory, 1959–1960: Part 3, Higher Education*. (Washington, D.C.: Government Printing Office, 1959), Table 4, p. 12.

Morrill Act of 1862 and related subsequent Acts of Congress." [2]

There are three major stages in the history of the American state university. In the first period, from the founding of the first quasi-public universities before 1800 to the Civil War, the major accomplishment was the establishment of the propriety of state-supported, lay-controlled, nonsectarian higher education. During the second phase, extending from about 1868 to about 1920, the curriculum was expanded from the bare essentials of undergraduate work to true university breadth through the emphasis on scholarly research and graduate study and the inclusion of professional schools within the structure of the university. The third stage, still in progress, is one in which a growing number of state universities have attained eminence among the great universities of the world. During the third phase also, a process of division is occurring through the establishment of semiautonomous campuses under a single Board of Regents (as in California), and of directly-controlled extension centers (as in the Wisconsin resident centers and the Pennsylvania Commonwealth Campuses).

Establishing the principle. The earliest state universities lacked many of the characteristics included in the present definition. Their curriculums approximated a secondary level of instruction rather than a collegiate or university level, and they did not pretend to offer specialized or advanced studies or to concentrate on research. They were privately controlled, and except for grants of state lands or similar endowments they were left to shift for themselves. In addition, the example of the church-related colleges in the colonies and the religious feeling of the people were so strong that several of these original state universities were at first under the control of sectarian boards of trustees, with clergymen as presidents.

Table 1 lists the 22 state universities founded before 1860, with the dates of their charters as listed in *American Universities and Colleges, 1960*. It must be remembered that several were established as private academies, seminaries, or colleges, and later came under state control and support. Nearly all were chartered for several years before they were able to offer their first collegiate instruction, and in

[2] S. V. Martorana and Ernest V. Hollis, *State Boards Responsible for Higher Education,* Office of Education Circular No. 619 (Washington, D.C.: Government Printing Office, 1960), p. 6.

most cases it was several decades before they were able to establish the first school or college other than Arts and Sciences to offer professional studies. Only in Maryland (established originally as a College of Medicine) and in Virginia (planned by the farseeing Thomas Jefferson) was professional education a part of the original plan. Pioneering institutions entered upon programs of law, medicine, or dentistry before the Civil War; only one engineering college—at Alabama—is listed before that event.

TABLE 1

CHARTER DATES AND EARLIEST PROFESSIONAL SCHOOLS IN 22 STATE
UNIVERSITIES FOUNDED BEFORE 1860

University	Charter Date	Earliest Professional Schools
Rutgers (New Jersey)*	1766	Engineering, Agriculture, 1864
University of Georgia	1785	Law, 1859
Unversity of North Carolina	1789	Law, 1845; Graduate School, 1876
University of Vermont*	1791	Medicine, 1822
University of Tennessee*	1794	Agriculture and Mechanics, 1869
University of South Carolina	1801	Pharmacy, 1865; Law, 1867
Ohio University	1804	Education, 1902
University of Maryland*	1807	Medicine, 1807; Dentistry, 1840
Miami University (Ohio)	1809	Education, 1902
University of Michigan	1817	Medicine, 1850; Law, 1859
University of Virginia	1819	Law, Medicine, 1819
Indiana University	1820	Law, 1838
University of Alabama	1820	Engineering, 1837; Law, 1845
University of Delaware*	1833	Engineering, Agriculture, 1870
University of Missouri*	1839	Education, 1868; Agriculture, Mines and Metallurgy, 1870; Law, Medicine, 1872
University of Mississippi	1844	Law, 1854
State University of Iowa	1847	Law, 1868; Medicine, 1870
University of Wisconsin*	1848	Law, 1868; Engineering, 1871
University of Utah	1850	Engineering, Mines and Mineral Industries, 1901
University of Minnesota*	1851	Medicine, Law, Dentistry, 1888
University of Florida*	1853	Agriculture, 1884
Pennsylvania State University*	1855	Agriculture, Engineering and Architecture, Mineral Industries, 1895

* Includes the land-grant function.

Source: Mary Irwin, ed., American Universities and Colleges, 8th ed. (Washington, D.C.: American Council on Education, 1960).

Land-grant legislation (to be discussed later in this chapter) had a stimulating effect on specialized education in the state universities as well as on separately established colleges. The process is summarized in a Report to the Governors' Conference:

> Breaches appeared here and there in the traditional framework of American higher education throughout the first half of the nineteenth century. Unceasing pressures forced new courses into the curriculum. A number of professional departments were established. But with each concession came demands for a dozen more, for the causes of pressures continued to mount. The nation's boundaries pushed all the way to the Pacific. Immense areas were opened for settlement. The rich agricultural lands of the Midwest were drawn closer to metropolitan markets through a network of railroads and waterways. Dramatic changes in the nation's economic fabric grew out of the industrial revolution. The demand for the greater democratization of higher education, first voiced decades earlier by Thomas Jefferson and others, now reached clamorous proportions. Thus the interaction of a wide variety of powerful economic, social, and political forces led to the creation in 1862 of the land-grant college system. So began the era of modern development in American higher education.[3]

The period of expansion.   The development of the state universities proceeded in response to the same forces. The 22 universities that had been established before the Civil War, and of course before the Morrill Act, established an additional 16 new professional departments between 1860 and 1880. As Midwestern and Western states were admitted to the Union, ten new state universities without land-grant functions were chartered between 1860 and 1900; at the same time, new state universities designated also as land-grant institutions were established in 16 states. These were in addition to the 37 separate land-grant colleges chartered during the same period. State-supported higher education during this post-Civil War period achieved several important milestones on the road to its present status:

1. The principle of regular tax-support for a major share of the costs of state-controlled higher education was accepted by all of the states.
2. The curriculum was expanded to include specializations and practical preparation for emerging professions and occupations.

---

[3] The Council of State Governments, *Higher Education in the Forty-Eight States* (Chicago: The Council of State Governments, 1952), p. 19.

3. The secularization of higher learning in the state-supported institutions won undisputed victory over the charges of godlessness and irreligion.

4. The elective system, or a combination of prescription and election, replaced the concept of a common curriculum and a single achievement for all college graduates.

5. The intellectual and spiritual aims of an education designed to inculcate Christian morality and good citizenship made way for the accumulative, empirical, practical, and frankly self-seeking aims of the new upwardly mobile middle-class student.

6. The growth of public secondary schools made it possible for greatly increased proportions of youth to aspire to and gain admittance to higher education.

Present status.   In 1962 there were 52 state universities of original establishment (including the "land-grant state universities"); all but four had been founded before the opening of the twentieth century. In 1962 their graduate schools and research programs were increasing to prepare for a crescendo of expansion. Their professional schools were growing in number, in variety, in enrollments, and, most important of all, in the quality of their faculties and in the scientific foundations of their instruction. Security in their support from public funds, together with legislative and constitutional guarantees of freedom, created a climate in which state universities could seek the facilities and faculties and students they needed to attain eminence.

Of these 52 state universities of original establishment, 30 are also the land-grant colleges of their states. In 1962 they enrolled almost 750,000 degree-credit students and included both students and faculty members from almost every country in the world and from every conceivable academic discipline. One of the universities was reputed to employ more Nobel prize winners in science than are found in the entire Soviet Union. Their faculties are engaged in research, both fundamental and applied, and are responsible for many of the salient characteristics, material and cultural, of American society.

Their successes are many and obvious. There are criticisms also of their less obvious shortcomings. These shortcomings include the universities' seeming failure to achieve permanent changes in the quality of intellectualism for many of their students; the divisive results of overspecialization and lack of communication among disciplines on the university campus; and the suspicion that students and instructors come to the campus in search of quite disparate values, and during their campus lives achieve only token and superficial formalized contacts with each other. The charge of isolated proximity is perhaps the most serious: that in their pursuit of the widening frontiers of learning, the faculties have forgotten or despised their parallel task of informing the young and of leading them on toward wisdom.

It is possible that state universities, in achieving their unwieldy enrollments and their enviable worldwide reputations, have drawn apart from the lives of the society that created them. They were established to perform limited and modest tasks in educating the young people of the commonwealth and in seeking answers to industrial and political problems. This seeking, though, leads them into the far reaches of human history, nature, and space, and so separates them from the daily lives of their students and of the enveloping community.[4]

An emerging concern of state universities is to find means of enhancing the understanding and support of their constituencies—by performing excellently the several tasks of undergraduate teaching, service research, professional preparation at the graduate level, and basic research. This plural objective is difficult, but need not be considered impossible.

The Land-Grant College and University

Section 4. *And be it further enacted,* that all moneys derived from the sale of the lands aforesaid by the states to which the lands are apportioned, and from the sales of land scrip hereinbefore provided for, shall be invested in stocks of the United States or of the States, or some other safe stocks, yielding not less than five per centum on the par value of said stocks; and that the moneys so invested shall constitute a perpetual fund, the capital of which shall remain forever undiminished (except so far as may be provided in section five of this act), and the interest of which shall be inviolably appropriated by each State which may take and claim the benefit of this act, to the endowment, support, and maintenance of at least one college where the leading object shall be, without excluding other

4 See Frank Pinner, "The Crisis of the State Universities: Analysis and Remedies," in Nevitt Sanford, ed., *The American College* (New York: John Wiley & Sons, Inc., 1962), Chap. 27.

scientific and classical studies, and including military tactics, to teach such branches of learning as are related to agriculture and the mechanic arts, in such manner as the legislatures of the States may respectively prescribe, in order to promote the liberal and practical education of the industrial classes in the several pursuits and professions in life.[5]

This provision of the Morrill Act of 1862 was the signal for the most rapid development of practical education in colleges and universities, but it had been preceded by a hundred years of discussion and advocacy. In early nineteenth century discussions of needed changes in existing patterns of higher education, several still familiar themes recur. Jonathan B. Turner of Illinois, for instance, was impatient with abstract and impractical education:

> How absurd would it seem to set a clergyman to plowing and studying the depredations of blights, insects, the growing of crops, etc., in order to give him habits of thought and mental discipline for the pulpit; yet this is not half as ridiculous, in reality, as the reverse absurdity of attempting to educate the man of work in unknown tongues, abstract problems and theories, and metaphysical figments and quibbles.[6]

In addition to the growing need for practical education to be made available more widely to the practical man, other influences impelled Senator Morrill to submit his land-grant proposal for colleges in every state. Public lands were being dissipated by donations to local and private interests; several of the states were unable to support higher education without federal assistance; European technical schools had demonstrated the benefits of agricultural and industrial education; and some political action seemed required to stimulate the support of farmers and workers in the Midwest and North for the Civil War effort.

The Morrill Act had immediate effect on the establishment of colleges in the states. Iowa had chartered a college in 1858, so it was the first to accept the conditions of the 1862 grant. Vermont followed in the same year, and within three years Massachusetts had divided its grant between the fledgling private Massachusetts Insti-

---

[5] The Morrill Act, 1862. Qnoted in Richard Hofstadter and Wilson Smith, *American Higher Education: A Documentary History,* Vol. II (Chicago: The University of Chicago Press, 1961), p. 568.

[6] Quoted in Edward D. Eddy, Jr., *Colleges for Our Land and Time* (New York: Harper & Row, Publishers, 1956), p. 25.

tute of Technology and the newly created Massachusetts Agricultural College. By 1865 also New York had joined with Ezra Cornell in the foundation of Cornell University, privately controlled and supported by both private endowments and land-grant funds, as "an institution in which any person can find instruction in any study."

By 1900, land grants had been assigned to 26 state universities, of which 16 were chartered after the passage of the Morrill Act. Separate colleges were chartered in 30 states during the same period.

Since 1900, only one separate land-grant college, now the Tennessee Agricultural and Industrial State University (1912), and four land-grant universities have been chartered—those in Puerto Rico (1903), Hawaii (1907), Alaska (1922), and the organization of the State University of New York in 1948 to include some part of the land-grant functions in that state. The degree-credit enrollments of land-grant colleges and universities of all these types in 1961 were reported to total 738,000. Of these enrollments, 473,000 were in state university land-grant institutions, and 265,000 were in separately organized land-grant colleges and universities.

During the early years of their existence, the separate institutions faced problems of enrollments and of curriculum. Although senators and farseeing college founders and presidents could see the need for the practical and liberal education of the industrial classes, the industrial classes were not convinced; engineering and mechanical studies prospered, but few students enrolled in agricultural courses. For one thing, there was no established body of science in agriculture. Many of the professors converted to agriculture from more classical subjects could have taught all that there was to teach in far less than a year. As time passed, research and experimentation remedied this lack. An additional obstacle in the path of the new colleges, both separately established and on university campuses, was the low prestige of practical subjects in the eyes of faculty and students in the older disciplines. This lack of prestige is being overcome by the land-grant institutions as they grow toward true university standing, but for most of their first century it posed a real problem in recruiting faculty and in maintaining the morale of students.

A hundred years after the Morrill Act of 1862, it was possible to recognize five basic principles of higher education that have been demonstrated in the programs of the land-grant colleges and universities:

1. The need for access to higher education by young persons from all walks of life, and of all degrees of wealth—the democratization of higher education.
2. The need for a broad diversification of curriculum, with some offerings that do not lead to degree objectives.
3. The relationship of the university to the life of its state and of segments of the population—business, industry, agriculture, homemakers, government.
4. The possibility of integrating teaching and research, to the marked advantage of both activities.
5. The concept of life-long education as expressed in extension activities and continuation study centers.

The land-grant colleges, then, have progressed toward the ideal enunciated by William O. Thompson at their fiftieth anniversary: "The tendency . . . to operate an institution for the sake of maintaining standards is all wrong as I see it. An institution is to be operated for the good it can do; for the people it can serve; for the science it can promote; and for the civilization it can advance." [7]

The Normal Schools and Their Successors

Many of the recent books about higher education have ignored the existence and history of the normal schools and of the state colleges and universities that have evolved from these beginnings. Yet these institutions are the most numerous class of all state higher education.

The first period in the development of normal schools is that from 1830 to the Civil War. This period coincides with the spread of public schools and the introduction of compulsory attendance in several of the states. The graduates of colleges at this period were unwilling and too few in number to care for the elementary instruction of children. Even when the high schools began to increase in size and number after the Civil War, the established state universities at first paid little attention to the preparation of teachers for them. The University of Missouri established a School of Education in 1868; there were normal departments at

---

[7] Quoted in Eddy, *op. cit.*, p. 269.

Kansas (1876), North Dakota (1884), and Nevada (1887), and a professor of education at Michigan by 1879. The University of South Carolina during its reorganization in 1882 established a School of Education, and the University of Washington had a College of Education by 1898. Outside of these scattered instances, the state universities were not greatly concerned with the preparation of teachers. The lack of interest on the part of the universities was as responsible as any other factor for the establishment of 100 normal schools between 1860 and 1899, and an additional 71 since 1900.

At the outset, these normal schools were not in any real sense institutions of higher education. They were established to train teachers for the elementary schools. Their courses of training typically ran from six weeks to an academic year, and their students were themselves recent graduates of elementary schools. From these limited beginnings, definite and inevitable steps have led them to their present status as multipurpose institutions of higher education.

The following brief history, taken from an institutional exhibit in *American Universities and Colleges,* was chosen as an example of the development in almost every state:

> College of liberal arts and teachers' college; coeducational; state control. Organized by Methodist Church as Mt. Vernon College 1855; offered to territorial government 1865 and accepted by first legislature of the State of Nebraska 1867 (first college in the state, and only one provided for by constitutional authority); name changed to Peru Normal College; first instruction 1867; name changed to Peru State Teachers' College and first baccalaureate degree awarded 1921; name changed to Peru State College 1949. Granting of liberal arts degree authorized 1949; master's degree in education authorized 1956. Accredited by North Central Association.[8]

The brief description indicates the several steps in the development of a comprehensive program. First, the normal school established a year-long training program in teaching skills and fundamentals to prepare elementary school graduates to teach in elementary schools. As high school graduates increased in number, the normal school began to require a high school diploma for admis-

---

[8] Mary Irwin, ed., *American Universities and Colleges,* 8th ed. (Washington, D.C.: American Council on Education, 1960), p. 628.

sion and to expand the course to two years by including more child study and a modicum of liberal education.

At this point, high school graduates began to apply for admission. These graduates were not interested in teaching, but they were willing to take preteaching courses as a price for the opportunity to continue their education. These students introduced a pressure to lengthen the course and to broaden its scope, at the same time that candidates for high school teaching positions were asking for the same kind of expansion in the curriculum. About this time, the normal schools began to change their names to "state teachers' colleges" and began to seek authorization to grant the bachelor's degree.

The rush of veterans to higher education at the end of World War II brought new peaks of enrollment to the state teachers' colleges, including many more students who desired not to teach but to become businessmen, scientists, or engineers, or to be prepared to continue graduate study. The next steps were inevitable: to expand the campus, to augment the library and laboratories, to add to the numbers and backgrounds of the faculty, and to prepare to seek authorization for a broad range of liberal arts majors. The change of name to "state college" came often as a recognition of a *fait accompli,* rather than as an expression of intention for the future.

But one step, in an expanding society, requires another. The needs of the schools for better-prepared teachers and for educational specialists, the needs of industry and business for increasing numbers of employees with advanced training, the need of youth for locally accessible higher education, and the interests and capacities of the newly recruited faculty members all combine to encourage the state colleges to offer graduate work in many subjects and to award the master's degree. At this point, they have become in fact (and more and more frequently in name) a species of state university, and they move to cap their admission to the company of higher education by doctoral and postdoctoral programs.

The 195 institutions that have shared in this lengthy and sometimes discouraging unfolding now enroll nearly 600,000 degree-credit students. The institutions range in size from only 200 or 300 students to more than 20,000. Their quality and their phase of development also vary, since some have still not reached the baccalaureate degree state, and others now grant earned doctorates of good quality and repute. Their history confirms once more the conclusion that in the United States the college of limited curriculum and specialized purpose is rapidly making way for the comprehensive college of many purposes and large enrollment.

The State-Controlled Junior College

Of approximately 400 public junior colleges in the United States, nearly all are controlled by local districts and supported partly by local taxes and partly by state subvention. There are, in addition, a number of two-year extension centers that are counted as part of the state universities in Pennsylvania, Wisconsin, and Indiana. These differ from the state-supported and controlled two-year colleges mainly in that direct control is exercised by the university, the budget is administered by the university, and the university affiliation is emphasized by name of the center and the nature of the instructional program. The state junior colleges have somewhat greater independence from the administrative officers of the university, although they may be under the same board of regents or trustees.

In Alaska, four community colleges have a joint control, not found elsewhere, in which the University Regents cooperate with the local school districts in operating the colleges. Their enrollments are reported as part of the enrollment of the University of Alaska. A two-year Agricultural and Mechanical College is found in Colorado, while Georgia has a series of seven special-purpose, two-year colleges that operate under the University System of Georgia. In Maryland, a different pattern of development has made St. Mary's Seminary Junior College—founded in 1839 as a school for young ladies —a state-controlled, coeducational, and multipurpose junior college, the only one of its sort in the state.

New Hampshire, New York, Oklahoma, and Oregon have two-year technical institutes, agricultural colleges, or agricultural and technical institutes controlled by state agencies, rather than by local agencies. New Mexico and Oklahoma have military two-year colleges, and New Jersey has a single state-controlled junior college. North Dakota has two-year Schools of Forestry and of Science under state control. Utah lists four junior colleges. Two are directly under state control; each of the others is controlled by one of the two state-controlled universities. West Virginia lists the Potomac

State College as being directly under the Board of Governors of the University, rather than under the University administration.

Altogether, these miscellaneous state-controlled junior colleges number 36, and enroll 26,000 degree-credit students. Their future development is not entirely clear, but it is safe to forecast that in most cases they will move as rapidly as enrollments and financial support permit to become four-year campuses with comprehensive curriculums, rather than toward the more usual pattern of the locally-controlled community junior college. Since they were established to meet conditions that now have changed, it is unlikely that most of these institutions will continue to exist as they now are. The Alaskan Community Colleges are already serving the needs of their local communities and are partly controlled by them. In the other states, a development toward four-year status seems a more likely prospect.

Other State-Controlled Higher Education

There are 61 state-controlled institutions of higher education that do not fit into any of the categories discussed previously. They were not established as the original state university, even though some of them share in its functions and a few have equal or greater prestige. They are not land-grant institutions, although several offer instruction in technological fields or in agriculture. They can be divided into six categories: former junior colleges, single-purpose institutions, women's colleges, former women's colleges, technical colleges, and a final group of seven otherwise unclassifiable institutions.

Former junior colleges. These eight colleges in five states were established during the twentieth century as two-year colleges, but were extended to baccalaureate-level instruction as enrollments and educational demand increased. The development of these institutions is the basis for the expectation that some of the other state-supported junior colleges may become four-year colleges as population grows in their respective states.

Single-purpose institutions. Seventeen specialized institutions have been separately established and titled. The students who enroll in each of these colleges have a common objective; and although several of them include in their curriculums a liberal requirement, their major emphasis is on a specific occupational competence. In the group are included three state medical colleges, three maritime academies, six schools of mining or of mining and technology, two military academies, two colleges of arts, and an academic and professional business college.

Women's colleges.   Colleges for women are disappearing from the scene of publicly-supported higher education, as are those limited to men students. Five still maintain the word in their title; two others began to accept male students only after World War II. All but one of the state women's colleges and former women's colleges were founded during the era of agitation for "rights for women" (1884 to 1908). Florida State University, formerly Florida State College for Women, was chartered in 1851. All of the state women's colleges are in southern states.

Technical colleges without land-grant assistance.   Thirteen of the states have established 22 separate technical or polytechnical colleges without land-grant assistance. Mostly established between 1890 and 1910, these colleges have developed their programs toward engineering and, in a few instances, toward a liberal arts emphasis. Their enrollments in 1962 ranged from 600 to more than 10,000 students.

Individually established colleges and universities.   Seven institutions do not fit into any of the categories described so far. They are not the original university of their states, but were established separately as multipurpose institutions. The oldest of these is The College of William and Mary, founded in Virginia in 1693; and the youngest (1962) is the University of South Florida, chartered in 1956. Wayne State University, established as a state-supported university in 1956 on the foundation of several municipal and private colleges dating back to 1868, is an example of adaptation and consolidation of existing colleges. Texas Southern University, established in 1947, was created as a university with its own board of trustees and administration.

A Summary of Trends

The detailed consideration of the history and scope of American state-supported and state-controlled higher education has served to highlight several trends that will influence the future development of these varieties of institutions. An inescapable observation is that since 1900 the growth in enrollment has been accommodated by expanding enrollments more than by establishing new institutions. In the sixty years prior to 1900, there were 219 new colleges established; since 1900 there have been only three-fifths as many new colleges (139), but enrollments have multiplied by ten. Since 1950 the growth in single-campus enrollment in several states has reached a limit, so that new campuses are being founded in significant numbers, especially in New York, California, Florida, and Michigan.

Another trend is to expand state support of higher education, not by authorizing new boards of regents and new independent special-purpose institutions, but by authorizing existing boards and institutions to establish new campuses, branches, or extension centers under the existing patterns of control. Indeed, several of the states have moved to bring previously independent institutions under more unified control and coordination.

The college of limited scope is changing to a multipurpose institution. The miscellaneous category (see page 15) described the last remaining few of the specialized colleges and universities. The emerging principle is that college-eligible youth should find an institution near their homes in which they can begin the pursuit of almost the entire spectrum of studies. Differentiation of institutional function in the future will be horizontal (that is, by levels of age of students and degrees granted) rather than vertical (that is, separating the vocational from the liberal, and professional training from research and general instruction).

In face of the growth in numbers of students and the complexity of curriculums, compounded by the growing similarity in scope of institutions of all types, the need for coordination of statewide effort in the field of higher education is becoming more apparent. Commonwealths cannot carry out their responsibility with economy and efficiency without constantly trying to avoid unnecessary duplication of effort.

The entire establishment of state-supported and controlled higher education was characterized by a Brazilian observer at the Centennial Convocation of the American Association of Land-Grant Colleges and Universities in 1961:

> This appears to me to be the special contribution of North America. With the Land-Grant Colleges the immense transformation was completed. The university built itself on the example of Bologna

and Salerno to exercise the function of professional training, on the example of Oxford and Cambridge to educate a gentleman, statesman, and administrator, on the example of Göttingen and Berlin to train the scholar and the research worker, on the example of Charlottenburg and Zurich to prepare the specialist, and on the example of the Land-Grant Colleges to devote itself to the application of science, the diffusion of knowledge, and the spirit of service. All these five functions, although accepted, are still to a certain degree in conflict within the universities. On the one hand, the attitude of unselfish devotion to culture, of a search for knowledge for its own sake; on the other, the contribution more specific of America in the position of urgent obligation to society, to make the university the means of selecting abilities for the most complete and varied training, a center for directing the march of progress for the whole society.[9]

Appendix A lists the state colleges and universities that existed in 1962, classified by type. The date of establishment and the degree-credit enrollment (1961) of each institution are also listed.

---

[9] Anisio S. Teixeira, "Forbears of the Revolutionary University," a speech delivered at the Centennial Convocation of the American Association of State Universities and Land-Grant Colleges, 1961.

CHAPTER II

Developmental Trends in
State Colleges and Universities

At the time of their first establishment, there were clear-cut and substantive differences in purpose and in curriculum among the various kinds of state institutions of higher education. Table 2 indicates the dates of establishment of the separate categories of colleges and universities; it is apparent that the period of most frequent establishment was the second half of the nineteenth century. More than half of the original state universities and of the teacher training institutions, and nearly all of the land-grant colleges date from this half-century. At this period in the history of higher education, each variety of state institution had its own special task.

TABLE 2

FOUNDATION OF STATE UNIVERSITIES AND COLLEGES,
BY TYPES AND BY HALF CENTURIES

Years	"Original" State Universities	Land-Grant Institutions (Separate)	Normal and Teachers' Colleges and Universities	State Junior Colleges	Miscellaneous Foundations	Total
Before 1800	5	—	—	—	1	6
1800–1849	13	—	11	1	5	30
1850–1899	30	40*	113	3	26	212
1900–1949	4	1	63	27	28	123
1950–	—	—	7	5	1	13
Total	52	41	194	36	61	384

* Includes Massachusetts Institute of Technology and Cornell University.

With the passage of time and the growth in national population and in student enrollments, many of the original differences among institutions have been obscured. Colleges of all sizes and origins are taking on the characteristics of the university and are attracting students of all kinds with widely varying purposes. Thus it is no longer possible to classify state colleges and universities into separate historical categories (see Chapter I). These developments bring to the fore three sorts of problems for public higher education: the problem of size, the problem of the appropriate diversification of curriculum, and the problem of coordination of effort.

Increasing Enrollments

Increasing enrollment is the most apparent problem of state universities and colleges. Expansion has been a constant characteristic of American higher education. Throughout American history, enrollments have risen much more rapidly than the population as a whole. For the near future, this trend will certainly continue.

Total enrollments in all types of institutions of higher education increased 16 times between 1900 and 1960; the proportion of the age-group 18 to 21 years of age who are enrolled in college rose during the same period from 4.01 per cent to 37.2 per cent, with the most rapid increases in the most recent years.[1] In addition, recent years have seen the publicly supported segment of higher education increasing more rapidly than the private segment, until in 1960 almost 60 per cent of all enrollments were in public colleges. Table 3 presents statistics for selected recent years to demonstrate this growth.

TABLE 3

TOTAL OPENING ENROLLMENT OF DEGREE-CREDIT STUDENTS IN FOUR-YEAR INSTITUTIONS, 1954, 1957, 1960, AND 1962

	TOTAL ENROLLMENTS	PUBLIC INSTITUTIONS		PRIVATE INSTITUTIONS	
		No.	Per Cent of Total	No.	Per Cent of Total
1954	2,183,943	1,131,000	51.8	1,053,000	48.2
1957	2,698,454	1,463,000	54.2	1,235,000	45.8
1960	3,156,390	1,742,000	55.2	1,414,000	44.8
1962	3,614,334	2,075,907	57.4	1,538,427	42.6

Source: Opening (Fall) Enrollment in Higher Education, 1962: Institutional Data, U.S. Office of Education Circular No. 697 (Washington, D.C.: Government Printing Office, 1962), Table 2.

[1] U.S. Bureau of the Census, Historical Statistics of the United States, Colonial Times to 1957 (Washington, D.C.: Government Printing Office, 1960), pp. 210–11; and Office of Education, Opening (Fall) Enrollment in Higher Education, 1960: Analytic Report, Office of Education Circular No. 652 (Washington, D.C.: Government Printing Office, 1961), p. 12.

It is possible to predict the size of the college age-group for as long as 18 years in the future, using the statistics of births in recent years. To derive from these predictions forecasts of college enrollments requires certain assumptions about the effective demand of young people for higher education, the stability of the economy, and the avoidance of natural or man-made catastrophies such as war or pestilence. All of the studies recently published agree that colleges and universities must prepare for much larger numbers of students over the decades of the 1960's and the 1970's. They differ in their assumptions about economic and demographic trends and, consequently, on their forecasts of the magnitude of the increases.

The study of Ronald B. Thompson [2] provides two extreme forecasts, one based on an assumption that the 1960 relation between the population aged 18–21 and college attendance will hold constant until 1978, and the other on a continuation of the trends of increase in enrollment during the decade of the 1950's. The second projection is much larger. Thompson's studies indicate that the nation as a whole must expect at least a doubling, and possibly a tripling, in college enrollments by 1978. The true figure will probably lie between these extremes. Table 4 presents projections for selected years based on both assumptions. Realization of even the smaller projection will strain the resources of the states in providing adequate higher education. In essence, it will require the duplication of all the buildings, libraries, laboratories, and other facilities, and almost all of the teaching staff, that have been developed since the founding of Harvard College in 1636—that is, doubling all of it

TABLE 4

PROJECTED DEGREE-CREDIT ENROLLMENTS IN HIGHER EDUCATION,
UNITED STATES, FOR SELECTED YEARS

	Projection A	Projection B
1960	3,569,071	——
1965	4,566,445	5,206,493
1970	5,455,625	6,816,095
1975	6,236,274	8,480,676
1978	6,410,827	9,217,217

Source: Ronald B. Thompson, *Enrollment Projections for Higher Education, 1961–1978* (Washington, D.C.: American Council on Education, 1961), p. 6.

---

[2] Ronald B. Thompson, *Enrollment Projections for Higher Education, 1961–1978* (Washington, D.C.: American Council on Education, 1961).

in a period of fifteen years. The independent colleges and universities will accommodate as much of the increase as their finances and their basic philosophy will allow, but the greatest share of the growth will be divided between the state institutions and the local junior colleges.

Diversification of Curriculum

The university pattern has served as a model and a goal for all other American public institutions of higher education. Over the years, each specialized institution has moved as rapidly as public support and legislative authorization would allow to undertake a complete and comprehensive program, in order that the students who came to any of the institutions for any educational reasons could find there curriculums appropriate to their purposes. This pressure for expansion in programs arose in part from emulation of the prestige of the university, but it received much more urgent stimulus from the need of larger numbers of young people to find educational opportunity near their homes. There is a tendency, as observed by Victoria McAlmon, for students "to accept the kind of public school instruction that is about." [3]

Students with no desire to teach enrolled in nearby normal schools, and entirely nonmechanical students attended land-grant colleges, simply because they were near and because it seemed logical to assume that one college ought to be much like another. The colleges responded to this implicit expectation by becoming as similar as possible. In so doing, they became aware of the inherent duality of some of their purposes.

General and specialized education. The conflict between specialized education and general education was one of the first problems to be faced in the expansion of both the university and of the professionally and technically oriented colleges. The private colonial college and university foundations were dedicated to general education. They attempted to prepare men by a classical curriculum for any of the responsibilities proper to a scholar and a gentleman. It is true that a large share of the early graduates of colonial colleges became ministers, but the colonial colleges were not professional

[3] Victoria McAlmon, "A New Type of College Training," *California Quarterly of Secondary Education,* No. 6 (October, 1930), 95–101.

schools. The graduate needed to pursue his pastoral studies independently or with an ordained minister after he had completed his college course. Other graduates turned with equal assurance toward the practice of politics or business, to reading law, or to an apprenticeship in medicine. The original state universities tended at first toward this general, preprofessional sort of educational program.

Most of the nonuniversity state institutions, on the contrary, were assigned a comparatively limited and specialized practical area of education; some of them prided themselves in their early years on avoiding any semblance of the intellectual or the cultural. The songs and traditions of a few of the land-grant colleges reflect this frontier attitude toward academic concerns. This divisive phase passed rather soon. Universities, normal schools, colleges of agriculture and mechanic arts, professional schools, and institutes of technology soon came to realize that to separate the education of doer and thinker, of worker and citizen, and of scientist and philosopher weakened and stultified both groups. In the past few years all institutions of public higher education have emphasized both aspects of a complete education: the vocational and the general.

This inherent duality of educational preparation was widely recognized in American higher education even before the Morrill Act gave it legislative expression in 1862. The founders of Rensselaer Polytechnic Institute in 1824 and of both the Lawrence and the Sheffield Scientific Schools in 1847 were convinced that other sorts of learning were needed. Russell Thomas presents evidence that at Amherst College in 1827 the classical course and the scientific course shared a "common core" of studies including mathematics, language, physical science, biological science, philosophy and religion, and history.[4] This experiment was abandoned after a few years, but it served to indicate that the first introductions of applied elements in higher education presented the general and the practical in combination, rather than in opposition.

With the establishment of land-grant colleges and the concurrent growth of graduate study in the universities, a sort of academic Gresham's law began to operate; and the specialized, the practical, and the vocational began to drive out the liberal, the humanistic, and the theoretical. Even students of traditionally general studies

---

[4] Russell Thomas, *The Search for a Common Learning* (New York: McGraw-Hill Book Company, Inc., 1962), p. 15.

such as literature and history succumbed to the lure of "the higher scholarship" and concentrated on philology and historiography, on research, and on development of new disciplines. The outcome of this concentration was not an unmixed blessing.

It is true that many of the most pleasant aspects of American life were made possible by the research and the narrow specialization of the universities since about 1850. Their contributions to health, to communication, to agriculture, to industrial productivity, and to control over nature in almost every aspect would have been impossible without dedicated and intensive specialization. The benefits of this concentration on research both to the quality of universities and to the material standard of living are so evident that both government and industry now subsidize professorial research by substantial annual contributions of money and materials. This activity will continue to be a part of the task of the American university, both public and private.

In the early decades of research development, however, the gains were costly. The sheer bulk of knowledge multiplied so rapidly that no man could longer aspire to master any major fraction of it. Courses in universities multiplied so rapidly that over 200 years would be needed for a student to complete, at an average rate of progress, all of the offerings of any major American university. The professor's attention was drawn from teaching to research and to publication, and the instruction of the undergraduate student was relegated to the graduate student or to the newly appointed and defenseless instructor. So far did specialization proceed that by 1930 President Coffman of the University of Minnesota could say, "It is no longer possible for a student to achieve a liberal education anywhere in the University."

General education, eclipsed for almost a century by the rising tides of research and of applied and professional education, returned to prominence in discussions of the college curriculum after World War I. This re-emergence was in many ways a reaction against the divisive forces of overspecialization, a return toward the basic, liberal, and unifying purposes of higher education.

General education is not conceived as a substitute for specialized education; rather, it is a complement. Both sorts are necessary to the preparation of a well-educated person in our society. The Morrill Act included both "the liberal and the practical education of the industrial classes" in its purposes. Although by 1920 liberal subjects had become increasingly specialized and illiberal, no responsible proponent of general education intended to displace specialization. Rather, recognition was asked for the concept that youth needed both kinds of preparation in order to participate effectively as educated men, as family members, as enlightened citizens, and as productive and competent workers.

The curricular arrangements proposed to satisfy these general needs ranged from a return to the classical curriculum of the early nineteenth century to the development of completely new combinations of concepts organized around the present educational needs of the students. The history of general education since 1920 is one of experimentation, of enthusiastic partisanship opposed by supercilious condemnation, of the extremes of too much and too little content, and of continuous and dedicated striving to find solutions to several educational problems that never had been faced before. Among these problems were the phenomenon of a third of the youth of college age enrolling in college, the doubling and redoubling of the amount of significant knowledge, and the increase in the length of time required to prepare for a life's work in a technically based economy.

Pure research. The best organization of the curriculum for general education and for specialized education has not yet been discovered, but the size of the problem only adds to the importance of finding a solution. One part of the difficulty grows out of another dualism in the American concept of state-supported higher education: the conflicting dedications to pure research and to service to society. Both activities invaded the campuses at about the same time, and ever since have shared facilities and the attention of faculties in uneasy rivalry with each other and in competition with the primary instructional responsibility.

The influence of American scholars returning from European study led to the establishment of state and private universities devoted to investigation and "pure" research. Their educational programs were based on the assumption that students had completed secondary education and were ready for independent and specialized study. Their faculties were recruited from men who had done significant research and who had been awarded the Ph.D. degree as a testimony of their investigative competence. Their ideal was the disinterested pursuit of truth without interference from selfish interests and without responsibility to achieve socially palatable or economically applicable findings.

This structure of graduate specialization and of intellectual independence, however, was imposed on an existing collegiate establishment that combined elements of secondary education and of scholarly specialization, that was committed by tradition and by capital investment to a college term of four years, and that had grown up, whether under public or private auspices, with strong commitments to sectarian religious influences. Graduate faculties were chosen from professors in the liberal arts colleges and were usually assigned some responsibility for undergraduate instruction. Students of undergraduate standing were in residence on almost every university campus. In addition, the university's concentration on research and publication with regard only to complete freedom of inquiry was broken at times by protests from powerful interests, whether political, economic, or religious.

Nonetheless, the record of the American universities in research has done credit to their German prototypes. The policies enunciated for the University of Chicago by its first president, William Rainey Harper, summarize the ideals of both the public and private universities:

> First, the ceaseless investigation of every realm of knowledge; second, an active ambition to put knowledge to use for human service; and third, a greater accessibility involving the maintenance of more ways of entrance to the university than had been true in the past and many more direct channels of communication with the outside world.[5]

Service to society. Harper's second ideal, the "service station concept," had been expressed through the separate establishment, during the same second half of the nineteenth century, of the colleges of agriculture and mechanic arts and the normal schools. Originally intended to provide a primarily practical education for workers in the emerging occupations of an industrial and technically controlled economy, these institutions found themselves forced into applied research in order to provide content for their newly created disciplines. Their concentration on practical research has been one

---

[5] John S. Brubacher and Willis Rudy, *Higher Education in Transition* (New York: Harper & Row, Publishers, 1958), p. 183.

cause of the phenomenal increases in American agricultural and industrial productivity over the last century. The change from an economy of scarcity to an economy of abundance derived an important impetus from land-grant college studies of such mundane problems as the relation of fertilizer to yield per acre, selective breeding of poultry for meat or for egg production, and the most efficient layout of factories to conserve time and motion. The expansion of the curriculum of secondary education was similarly encouraged by the studies conducted in normal schools and teachers' colleges.

Theoretically, the universities should have been satisfied with pure research, and the applied colleges with their assistance to the farmer, the industrialist, the homemaker, the businessman, and the schoolman. Nevertheless, two forces operated to expand the functions of both kinds of institutions. The faculty in the colleges and institutes began to envy the status of university faculties. As the number of technical college faculty members with earned doctorate degrees from the universities increased, they brought the values and the interests of their graduate professors to their own campuses. Some of their applied researches raised fundamental questions of cause and nature—questions which were unlikely to yield immediately rewarding answers but which were irresistibly attractive in their challenge to the trained scholar. In addition, in states where the university and the applied colleges existed separately, the desire for status caused the faculties of the more limited institutions to aspire to equal support and standing. Where the university was also the land-grant institution, and shared the campus with the applied subjects, even more powerful and subtle influences moved the faculties in agriculture, engineering, and education toward fundamental, rather than immediately useful, research.

The universities at the same time were under pressure to take on applied research. Public support of the professional colleges, engendered by success of their services to their states, began to be felt in annual legislative budget sessions. The specialized knowledge and competence of the university faculty were recognized by leaders in business and industry, especially as more and more of these leaders were themselves college graduates. Looking back, it seems inevitable that the several varieties of public institutions should become more and more similar, by accepting the dual responsibilities for pure research and for service to their constituencies and by coming to realize that their tasks are not truly competitive, but rather are complementary aspects of the same unending quest.

Serving undergraduate and graduate students. President Harper's third ideal, that of "greater accessibility," has led to an additional dualism in state-supported higher education: the distinction between the transmission of the culture on the college level and its extension through graduate study. The educational needs of freshmen and sophomores as recipients of the interpretation of knowledge are somewhat different from those of upper-division and graduate students. Each group requires different purposes, methods, and content. When freshmen are taught as graduates should be taught, or vice versa, the quality of higher education suffers. Yet the confusion of purposes and techniques is hard to avoid when both groups are enrolled on the same campus and study under the same professor. It was this diversity of aims that led Henry Tappan to conclude as early as 1851 that "there is nothing wrong with the university that would not be set right if it could be freed of its 'swollen fortune' of freshmen students."

American state colleges and universities are committed to these cross purposes and diverse functions. The idea of a single aim and a concentrated effort for each institution may be appealing, but diversification is both the destiny and the opportunity of higher education. Fewer and fewer state colleges and universities are now limited to a single area of professional training, and more and more of them are expanding in enrollments and in curriculums toward true university status.

One of the consequences of this recent trend toward overlapping and expansion of roles has been a competition within states for position and support. When both the "University of the State" and the "State University" have strong alumni associations, excellent faculties and academic reputations, large enrollments, and successful athletic programs, the legislature may find it difficult to decide on levels of support for each institution. Added to this competition is the rapid development of curriculums and enrollments in the former normal schools and the forecasts of doubling and tripling numbers of college-age youth. The need for statewide, regional, and national planning and coordination is apparent.

The Need for Coordination

For a very few decades after their first establishments, a comfortable pattern of diversification of function was accepted by the several kinds of state institutions. The normal schools trained teachers; the agricultural colleges taught farmers and extension workers; and the university educated professors and professionals. There were, and still are, pressing problems of the appropriate kind of governmental direction and budgetary control for each sort of institution, but the planning and coordination of their competing efforts were rarely considered in legislative halls. Recently, however, the problems of enrollment and the problems of diversification of function have created additional problems of coordination. From 1957 through 1960, long-term planning and coordination were considered by at least 25 state legislatures in enactments providing for some type of statewide survey of the facilities, finances, programs, or administration of higher education.[6]

Yet coordination of higher education, necessary as it may seem from a fiscal or political point of view, can threaten many of the distinctive qualities and achievements of state institutions. Extensive autonomy has enabled some of them to achieve eminence among the universities of the world at the same time that institutions in other states under tight legislative control were perpetuating mediocrity, rote learning, and the trappings of culture without its essence. Higher education must be a creative activity or it is nothing. Some order, however, must be introduced into the chaos of competing institutions and systems of higher education within a state, or none of its colleges and universities can attain or maintain the excellence that is essential to the continued well-being of the commonwealth. The problem then becomes one of finding the optimum reconciliation of the opposing forces of autonomy and coordination.

In his report on the several patterns of coordination that existed in 1956–57, Glenny stated several assumptions that he considered basic to the evaluation of these patterns:

---

[6] Ernest V. Hollis, William G. Land, and S. V. Martorana, *Survey of State Legislation Relating to Higher Education, January 1, 1960 to December 31, 1960,* Office of Education Circular No. 647 (Washington, D.C.: Government Printing Office, 1961), p. 8.

1. Diversification of educational opportunity is desirable; uniformity and rigidity are undesirable.

2. A measure of freedom and initiative of individual institutions within each state benefits education.

3. The society benefits by maximum extension of higher educational opportunities appropriate to the varying interests and ability levels of the youth of the state and the needs of society.

4. College enrollments will increase at about the rates which have been predicted by the responsible agencies within the several states.

5. Higher educational institutions must make more effective use of every dollar, avoiding inferior quality in programs, inadequate numbers of programs and institutions, wasteful administrative practices, and unnecessary duplication of educational functions and facilities.

6. An ideal administrative model for state coordination of higher education is not now known.

7. Some kind and degree of coordination of public institutions is desirable and inevitable either through the legislature, state budget and fiscal authorities, or some board or voluntary council especially established for this purpose.[7]

Glenny's assumptions underline several causative aspects of the trend toward the establishment of coordinating agencies for higher education. Rising expenditures for higher education and the resulting desire of legislatures to effect economies bring about one set of pressures for coordination. Between 1930 and 1960, total expenditures for higher education rose from 0.6 per cent of the Gross National Product to 1.3 per cent. In dollars, the rise was even more rapid, because of the decline in the purchasing power of the dollar. This comparative doubling of the share of higher education in the national income emphasized the need for economy. At the same time, projected increases in the size of the college-age group and in the proportions of these youth attending college made it evident that regardless of all efforts toward economy, higher education would require an increasing share of the national income at least over the next two decades.

Another force is felt in states with several kinds of state institutions and especially in those with several systems of colleges. Here the need for criteria for equating costs and for allocating funds equitably has led to the establishment of coordinating agencies. In these states also it has been recognized that all the institutions should

---

[7] Lyman A. Glenny, *Autonomy of Public Colleges: the Challenge of Coordination* (New York: McGraw-Hill Book Company, Inc., 1959), p. 6.

attempt to perform some basic and common functions excellently, while expensive and unnecessary duplication of specialized curriculums with small enrollments should be avoided. The operation of this principle has seemed to depend more on external coordination than on complete institutional autonomy. It has even been reported that undignified lobbying by competing institutions has stimulated the establishment of coordinating agencies by more than one legislature.[8]

Glenny notes, however, that the soundest justification for coordination is its possible contribution to the improvement of the quality of all higher education within a state and to the development of a reasonable and comprehensive system of institutions. Unfortunately, he found only two states (in 1957) that had even mentioned this purpose in their laws. Most coordinating agencies were established to eliminate duplication and to control competition between institutions, rather than to make possible the achievement of high standards of education for large numbers of young people.

Varieties of Coordinating Agencies

At their first establishment, state institutions are usually governed by *independent* governing boards, each charged with control and operation of a single institution. As an example, in 1804 the State of Ohio established the Board of Trustees of the Ohio University; in 1809, the Board of Trustees of Miami University; and in 1870, the Board of Trustees of the Ohio State University. Similar separate boards, each with authority over a single institution, have been established for the other three state institutions of higher education: Bowling Green State University, Central State College, and Kent State University.

A *coordinating-governing board* is one that governs a group of institutions with similar functions and that coordinates their activities and expansion by control over budgets, establishment of new campuses, expansion of programs, and broad elements of institutional policy. Examples of this sort of board are the Board of Regents of the University System of Georgia (established in 1931

---

8 For example, see T. R. McConnell, *A General Pattern for American Public Higher Education* (New York: McGraw-Hill Book Company, Inc., 1962), pp. 138–40.

and given constitutional status in 1943) and the Board of Trustees of the California State Colleges (1960).

Two types of coordinating efforts without governing authority have been established, one by voluntary agreement of the independent institutions involved and the other by statutory enactment. Examples of *voluntary coordination* are found in Ohio and Indiana. In each of these states the coordinating council is made up of officers of the agreeing institutions, and each officer is free to cooperate or to withdraw if he feels unable to accept any decision of the group. The virtues of this sort of coordination inhere in the need to reach solutions by agreement rather than by legislation, and in the first-hand knowledge that the members of the board have of the problems of their several institutions. The preservation of the autonomy of each independent institution is another major value in this pattern of coordination. Its weakness, of course, is that in important conflicts of interest it is all too easy for the member institutions to protect their own established practices rather than to re-evaluate them in light of emerging conditions. The strengths, however, outweigh the weaknesses when men of good will and mutual esteem work together for voluntary coordination, but critics of this plan seek a greater certainty that coordination will continue under all conditions. Glenny suggests also that this plan seems unlikely to work well for more than six or seven institutions in one grouping, or for very long periods of time.[9]

Statutory coordinating boards exist in nine states in which separate governing boards direct and control one or more institutions each. These coordinating boards have varying degrees of authority to regulate, organize, or recommend policy affecting the functions of program development, budget requests, or institutional planning; but they do not control the operation of the institutions. Examples of the coordinating board are the New Mexico Board of Educational Finance (1951), the Council on Public Higher Education in Kentucky (1952), the Council of Higher Education for Virginia (1956), and the California Coordinating Council for Higher Education (1960).

The Coordinating Council of Higher Education in Utah was established at a time when it was possible to capitalize upon the experiences of the coordinating agencies then operating in other

9 Glenny, *op. cit.,* pp. 248–56.

states and, at the same time, to include new emphasis and new functions for such bodies. Portions of the legislation enacted to establish the council reflected the new directions for coordinating councils. The legislation contained many repetitions of the expression "public post-high school educational institutions"; and the council was empowered to give leadership "to the end that an efficient and effective state system of post-high school education may be more fully developed and maintained." [10]

In other respects, the Utah statute reflected the duties commonly performed by these new agencies. It included a statement of educational purpose, as well as provision for study and recommendation of budgets; it established a lay coordinating board, but with representation of the institutions to be coordinated; it protected the autonomy of the several institutions, but did assure the state that requested budgets would be adequate but not duplicating, and that planning for the future needs of higher education would be both continuous and competent.

Summary

Faced by the prospect of rapidly increasing numbers of students at the undergraduate and graduate levels, state-supported universities and colleges have been undergoing a period of re-examination of their purposes. The result has been a movement of all kinds of state post-high school educational institutions toward a comprehensive curriculum, combining on each campus research and service to the state, specialized and general education, and undergraduate and graduate programs. As institutions within each state that were once quite disparate in their nature become more similar, however, the need arises for coordination of their efforts without interference with their capacity to achieve excellence through the creative efforts of their own faculty members. These considerations have brought about the establishment recently in several states of coordinating councils for higher education.

---

[10] Quoted from William F. Edwards and John T. Wahlquist, *A Proposed Coordinating Council of Higher Education for Utah* (Salt Lake City, Utah: State of Utah Coordinating Board of Higher Education, 1958), p. 2.

CHAPTER III

Programs of State Colleges and Universities

The American system of higher education is so unsystematic and so highly diversified in history, purpose, stage of development, and predominant student culture that it is difficult to state any fully defensible single thesis about the curriculum of the entire group of institutions. Still, these institutions are moving inexorably toward greater similarity; they must share responsibility for a common basic education for their students at the same time that each of the major classes of institution continues to improve and extend its own unique sector of the entire pattern of state higher education.

The General Undergraduate Curriculum

The first objective of the American colleges was to transmit the culture to the oncoming generation through a limited and prescribed course of studies that all students completed together. Two conditions that made possible this tidy and manageable pattern of instruction no longer exist: the small body of knowledge that was worth transmitting, and the small number of young people who could afford and who desired to pursue this liberalizing introduction to knowledge. Increasing numbers of qualified and aspiring college applicants have brought new expectations to bear on curricular developments, and the bulk of important and available knowledge has increased as rapidly, or even more rapidly, than the student body. It is certain that not even the ablest student can aspire to master all knowledge, or even to sample all of it judiciously.

Awareness of these two increases has caused concern about the selection of instructional content and of students. If not all knowledge can be taught, what knowledge is of most value? If not all applicants can be accepted, on what bases can selection be made? Is it possible that some kinds of knowledge are more appropriate for some kinds of students? If this be true, are there any techniques for matching the student appropriately to the curriculum? If such techniques are developed, how then do institutions ensure that they do not create a new set of chauvinisms, based on loyalties to the language, the terrain, and the mysteries of academic disciplines?

Indeed, it became apparent very early in the twentieth century that exactly this sort of alienation was taking place and that college attendance resembled the naturalization procedures for the citizens of competing and unrelated professional specialties, rather than initiation to the fullness and universality of humanistic understanding.

Several strategies were suggested to counteract the divisive effect of overspecialization. The first was the counsel of retreat. In an earlier day, this problem of separation of disciplines did not arise. The remedy for emerging dispersion seemed clear to conservative educators. They advocated a return to the tried and true, to the eternal truths, and to the single college experience. They felt that all graduates would thus have much in common before they pursued their separate ways in specialized studies. Undergraduate education, in this view, should concentrate on abstract study in languages, literature, philosophy, and natural science.

Another strategy suggested a recognition of the importance of the developing disciplines. It proposed that all men need basic understanding of the principles of all areas of knowledge; that the undesired side effects of specialization can be avoided if all men are introduced to the important methods and conclusions of all disciplines prior to their concentrated study of a single field; and that a series of concentrated or survey courses would enable students to achieve this kind of introductory knowledge.

A third approach was to minimize the importance of overspecialization and to suggest that a solution could be developed without drastic action. This approach stressed that the departmental organization of the university and of the curriculum is fundamental and inherent in the nature of knowledge. The problem, in this view, arose not from the growth of specialization, but from the elective principle that allowed students to choose their own courses as they wished. If the students' lack of knowledge could be controlled through requirements for distribution of studies, the whole problem could be solved.

None of the patterns—return to great books, synthesis, or required distribution—has proved to be an adequate solution to the still persisting need to build into higher education a unifying and integrating force to complement and counteract the antihumanistic forces that are associated with specialized study. It seems unfair and unnecessary to qualify specialization always as "narrow" or "excessive"; it should be sufficient to realize that specialization is not in itself a complete education for human beings, that it ought to be complemented by efforts to protect the right of all undergraduates to obtain general as well as specialized knowledge and to participate in the benefits of their culture as well as to extend its boundaries.

State colleges and universities recognize their obligation to contribute in this manner to the general education of their students. Even though most of these institutions were established to serve a narrowly defined and immediate practical need, most now offer comprehensive curriculums and emphasize basic requirements in general education. Nevertheless, it seems to be true that, with only a very few exceptions, these colleges have been more imitative than creative in their search for patterns of general education.

In his recent study of general education since 1800, Thomas [1] included descriptions of only five programs in state colleges and universities: those at Michigan State University, The University of Minnesota, The University of Oregon, San Francisco State College, and Washington State University. Others of these colleges require organized patterns of courses as a contribution to general education; but it is more often the private, rather than the public, college that has been able to inaugurate curricular innovations designed to challenge the best efforts of both students and faculty in their joint search to rediscover the values of a liberal education.

Undergraduate Specializations

Several powerful trends contributed to the transformation of the college curriculum from a rigid concentration on classical subjects to emphasis on the practical and the immediate concerns of the students. Not the least of these trends was the rapid increase in the breadth and the depth of human knowledge that made it impossible

---

[1] Russell Thomas, *The Search for a Common Learning: General Education, 1800–1960* (New York: McGraw-Hill Book Company, Inc., 1962).

for any student to study all of the worthwhile subjects. Realistically, worthwhile intensity of study and the need to extend the horizons of learning through research force scholars to specialize.

The continuous spread of technology in industry and agriculture was another of the forces that contributed to the development of specialized curriculums. First, in the professions of law and medicine and then, in natural science, business and agriculture, and social sciences and government, the wise application of new insights to the solution of practical problems fostered the pursuit of depth in study and worked against the former ideal of breadth. Eells and Haswell [2] list more than 2400 different degrees conferred by American universities and colleges, and almost 3000 abbreviations for them. The extent of available undergraduate specialization is indicated by a very brief selection of baccalaureate titles from the entire list:

A. B. in J.	(Journalism)
Ag. E.	Agricultural Engineer
B. A. A.	Bachelor of Applied Arts
B. Des.	Bachelor of Design
B. G. E.	Bachelor of Geological Engineering
B. Gen. Ed.	Bachelor of General Education
B. S. F. M.	Bachelor of Science in Forest Management
B. S. F. Mgt.	Bachelor of Science in Fisheries Management
B. S. F. T.	Bachelor of Sciences in Fuel Technology
B. Sc. in Rest. Mgt.	Bachelor of Science in Restaurant Management
Sch. Mus. B.	Bachelor of School Music

American Universities and Colleges [3] includes in its institutional exhibits a listing of departmental specializations offered in each institution. Inspection of the descriptions of six of the largest state universities and colleges made possible the following listing of 73 specializations. Some, such as Scandinavian, were offered in only one of the universities; the basic subjects like English and physics were offered in all. The list, incomplete as it is, is impressive evidence of the extent of the specialization available in state institutions.

---

[2] Walter C. Eells and Harold A. Haswell, *Academic Degrees: Earned and Honorary Degrees Conferred by Institutions of Higher Education in the United States* (Washington, D.C.: Government Printing Office, 1960).

[3] Mary Irwin, ed., *American Universities and Colleges,* 8th ed. (Washington, D.C.: American Council on Education, 1960).

Undergraduate Specializations Offered in One or More of
Six Large State Colleges and Universities

Accounting	Foreign Studies	Nursing
Advertising	General Engineering	Occupational Therapy
Aeronautics	Geography	Pharmacy
Agriculture	Geology	Philosophy
Anthropology	German	Physical Education
Architecture	Health and Hygiene	Physics
Art	History	Police Science
Astronomy	History of Art	Political Science
Bacteriology	Home Economics	Psychology
Biology	Humanities	Public Health
Botany	Industrial Arts	Real Estate
Business Administration	Industrial Engineering	Recreation
Business Education	Industrial Relations	Religion
Chemical Engineering	Interdisciplinary Studies	Romance Languages
Chemistry	Journalism	Scandinavian
Civil Engineering	Library Science	Science Education
Classical Studies	Management	Secretarial Administration
Drama	Marketing	Slavic Languages
Economics	Mathematics	Social Work
Education	Mechanical Engineering	Sociology
Electrical Engineering	Mineralogy	Speech
English	Mineral Industries	Statistics
Entomology	Music	Technology
Far Eastern Languages	Near Eastern Studies	Theatre Arts
		Zoology

The Morrill Act of 1862 and succeeding similar enactments, encouraging by federal grants and subsidies the study of useful applications of research, have contributed directly to the increase in undergraduate specialization. Indeed, the separately established land-grant colleges, like the normal schools and teachers' colleges, were founded in order to provide for specialized study. They have achieved a measure of generality in their offerings through imitation of the liberal arts colleges and universities, at the same time as these latter institutions were forsaking some of the former breadth of requirements in conformity with the popular demand for specialized courses.

This popular demand has been an additional potent influence on the development of specialization within the public universities and colleges. Dependent for their support on annual or biennial appropriations by legislators, these institutions have been forced to serve the needs of their constituencies by instituting courses, departments, or even schools that the established faculties deplored and that administrative officers would have preferred to see established elsewhere, or not at all.

Even so, specialization has not been without proponents and defenders in higher education. The objections of Benjamin Rush, Benjamin Franklin, and Thomas Jefferson to the sterility for most citizens of the classical curriculums, and their proposals for applied and meaningful courses, have been cited frequently. Philip Lindsley, in 1832, deplored the limitation of learning to the professional classes, and he pleaded the cause of the farmer and the mechanic who needed to be educated if they were to forestall complete control of government by the lawyer. He stated, "I look forward to the period when it will not be deemed anti-republican for the college graduate to follow the plough; nor a seven days' wonder for the labourer to be intellectual and to comprehend the Constitution of his Country." [4]

The people of Wisconsin fully espoused the concept that the state university existed to serve the people of the state through research into their problems and instruction in occupational fields important to them. As early as 1858, the state senate felt that the university should be adapted to popular needs and offer courses to meet the wants of the greatest number of citizens, in order to fit them for their pursuits in life. Although this intimate involvement of the state university with the daily life of its commonwealth has been derided as a "service station" ideal, in Wisconsin the results have enabled the university to achieve renown as an institution of scholarship and, at the same time, to contribute tangibly to the quality of government and to the health of the economy.[5]

In a different way, the example of the German universities, greatly admired by American scholars during the nineteenth century, added impetus to the increasing specialization of the college curriculum. The ideals of meticulous research and of scholarly publication in the graduate schools were transmitted to doctoral candidates, who then went forth to serve as faculty members in the colleges. This sort of highly specialized teacher had two influences on the college curriculum. His own interests were concentrated on the specialized field in which his major research was done, and this interest could not help

---

[4] Quoted in Richard Hofstadter and Wilson Smith, *American Higher Education: A Documentary History*, p. 377.

[5] See Richard Hofstadter and C. DeWitt Hardy, *The Development and Scope of Higher Education in the United States* (New York: Columbia University Press, 1952), pp. 44–48.

affecting his choice of class material and his decisions in matters of departmental policy. Beyond that, the research man knew the skills that would be most useful to those of his students who would become graduate students, doctoral candidates, and college professors. He tended to develop patterns of undergraduate requirements to produce those skills. One result was that the student began his professional or preprofessional courses earlier and dropped many of the liberal and nonspecialized subjects.

All the pressures toward undergraduate specialization have encouraged state universities and colleges to build strong departments in all areas of learning so that they may contribute to the welfare of the state and the nation and achieve sound reputations for scholarly excellence. In addition, the results of their research have had beneficial application in almost every aspect of the national life.

For the individual student, however, the pressures toward specialization and the resulting prescription of the greatest part of his program have not always been happy. Too often these pressures have caused students to be given training when they sought education, and to substitute skills for wisdom. In their zeal to encourage research, professors have sometimes overlooked the fact that the scholar of today needs both depth and breadth of culture. The college years may be the student's last chance for organized pursuit of breadth, whereas many kinds of employment provide lifelong encouragement to deeper specialization.

In recent decades, therefore, colleges have sought curricular arrangements through which breadth of learning may be achieved without jeopardizing the quality of scholarly preparation for specialization. The patterns of undergraduate education are one aspect of this search. A more promising trend may involve the lengthening of the usual four-year college term to allow students to be exposed to a greater share of the wealth of pertinent learning. This trend is reflected in graduate enrollments, which increased from 5831 in 1900 to 278,603 in 1957. This is almost a fifty-fold increase. During the same period, undergraduate enrollments grew from about 238,000 to 3,000,000, an increase of about 13 times the earlier figure. A recent study of college seniors in 135 colleges showed that 77 per cent of them hoped to continue into graduate school, and that 20 per cent had completed plans to do so in the fall after their graduation.[6] This trend if it continues, may provide a realistic solution to the dilemma of breadth versus depth in undergraduate education.

Graduate Study

True graduate education in the United States began just a century ago. Before that time, doctoral degrees had been awarded to honor men of achievement, but not in recognition of a planned program of supervised advanced study and research. The first three earned American doctorates were granted in 1861 by Yale. In 1876, the number of doctorates had grown to 18, granted by eight universities.

> Not until the beginning of the twentieth century did graduate education become a significant activity of the colleges and universities of the United States. . . . The development of Johns Hopkins University (founded in 1876) was followed by the establishment of graduate schools at Columbia University in 1880, Clark University and Catholic University in 1889, Harvard University and University of Chicago in 1890, and Yale University in 1892. Three state universities had joined this group before the turn of the century—the University of Wisconsin in 1892, the University of Nebraska in 1895, and the University of Kansas in 1896.[7]

There were several state institutions before this period that used the name "university," but without offering studies beyond the bachelor's degree that were intended to culminate in a doctorate.

During its hundred years of history, American graduate education has evoked criticism from several qualified observers. Some of the criticism is generated by the continuing adaptation of graduate curriculums to emerging needs for professional training, from a lessening emphasis on humanistic studies in the doctoral program and an increased emphasis on the applied and practical. Within graduate faculties themselves there is uncertainty about the purposes of graduate work, whether it is for application or for theory, for tradition or for today. Both points of view are reflected in requirements for the degree at different graduate schools and, sometimes, even within the divisions of the graduate school within a single university. So

---

[6] James A. Davis and Norman Bradburn, *Great Aspirations: Career Plans of America's June 1961 College Graduates* (Chicago: National Opinion Research Center, 1961), p. 37.

[7] Kenneth Little, "Graduate Education," in *Encyclopedia of Educational Research*, 3rd ed. (New York: The Macmillan Company, 1960), p. 594.

long as both points of view attract articulate proponents, there will be adverse criticism of graduate education from both camps.

The trend has been in the direction of applied knowledge. Between 1897 and 1957 the proportion of graduate students in the humanities dropped from 48 per cent to 15 per cent, while the social sciences increased from 23 to 36 per cent, the biological sciences from 10 to 17 per cent, and the physical sciences from 19 to 32 per cent. Even more illuminating is the listing of fields for graduate study, partial though it is, in a supplement to *A Guide to Graduate Study*.[8] It is reproduced to demonstrate a part of the diversity of studies that may be pursued in American graduate schools. It should be noted further that these lists are of major fields leading to the Ph.D. degree. The number of advanced degrees, and the criticisms of them, indicate that there is need for a consensus of university practice on the scope of graduate study. Either an increasing number of specialized doctorates should be encouraged, or common definitions of purpose should be agreed upon as a basis for limiting the increase in titles.

The demand for holders of doctoral degrees continues to rise. Noneducational occupations employ about 40 per cent of the doctor's degree graduates who enter new occupations; teaching positions attract about 43 per cent; and nonteaching educational service accounts for the remaining graduates. The competition for these highly trained specialists is keen. This is one of the major reasons graduate education will probably increase as a function of state universities. The need for new college teachers is estimated to increase from 29,000 in 1961 to 36,000 in 1970 [9] (and noneducational employment of Ph.D.'s will increase at least as rapidly) but the annual supply amounts to only a fraction of the needed number. In 1958–59, fewer than 10,000 doctorates of all sorts were awarded, 4,800 by public universities and 4,500 by private ones.

Faced with this constantly increasing disparity between supply and demand, educational authorities in the states will take steps to increase the supply. Among steps suggested have been an increase in

---

[8] *Major Fields for Graduate Study Leading to the Ph.D. Degree,* a supplement to *A Guide to Graduate Study* (Washington, D.C.: American Council on Education, 1958).

[9] Research Division, National Education Association, *Teacher Supply and Demand in Universities, Colleges, and Junior Colleges, 1959–60 and 1960–61* (Washington, D.C.: National Education Association, 1961), pp. 43, 56.

MAJOR FIELDS FOR GRADUATE STUDY LEADING TO THE PH.D. DEGREE

1. *In the Humanities*
   Architecture
   Classical Languages
   Comparative Literature
   English
   Fine Arts
   French
   German
   Italian
   Journalism
   Linguistics
   Music
   Philosophy
   Portuguese
   Religion
   Russian
   Spanish
   Speech and Dramatic Arts
   Foreign Languages, Other:
     Near Eastern Languages
     Oriental Languages
     Romance Philology
     Indic and Far Eastern Languages
     Celtic
     Semitic Languages
     American Indian Languages
     East European Languages
     African Languages
     Far Eastern Languages
     Rumanian
     Slavic Languages
     Dutch
     Scandinavian
     Arabic, Persian, Turkish Languages
     Sanskrit
     Chinese
     Japanese
     Uralic and Altaic Languages
     Hebrew
     Polish
     Egyptian
   Humanities, Other:
     Communications
     Inter-departmental Program
     History of Culture
     Early Christian Literature
     Folklore
     Aesthetics of Literature
     Franciscan Studies
     Humanities for College Teaching

2. *In the Biological Sciences*
   Agriculture
   Anatomy
   Bacteriology
   Biochemistry
   Biology
   Biophysics
   Botany
   Entomology
   Forestry
   Genetics
   Home Economics
   Medical Specialties
   Pharmaceutical Science
   Physiology
   Psychology
   Public Health
   Veterinary Medicine
   Wildlife Management
   Zoology
   Biological Sciences, Other:
     Dentistry
     Gnotobiotics
     Institution Management
     Hospital Administration
     Forensic Pathology
     Conservation
     Fisheries
     Human Variation
     Resource Management
     Tanning Research
     General Science
     Range Management

MAJOR FIELDS FOR GRADUATE STUDY LEADING TO THE PH.D. DEGREE *(cont.)*

3. *In the Physical Sciences*

Astronomy
Chemistry
Engineering:
 Aeronautical
 Agricultural
 Ceramic
 Chemical
 Civil
 Electrical
 Industrial
 Mechanical
 Metallurgical
 Mining
 Petroleum
 Irrigation
 Instrumentation
 Marine
 Wood Technology
 Engineering Administration
 Fuel Technology
 Petroleum and Natural Gas
 Sanitary
 General Engineering
Geography
Geology
Mathematics
Meteorology
Oceanography
Physics
Statistics
Physical Sciences, Other:
 City Planning
 Milling Industry
 Crystallography
 History of Science
 Science College Teaching
 Solid State Science
 Optics
 Applied Science
 General Science
 Industrial Administration
 Physical Sciences

4. *In the Social Sciences*

Anthropology
Business and Commerce
Economics
Education
Foreign Area Studies
History
International Relations
Library Science
Political Science
Social Work
Sociology
Social Sciences, Other:
 American Studies
 Medieval Studies
 Social Sciences, General Law
 Interdisciplinary Program in
  Liberal Arts
 Social Thought
 American Civilization
 Child Welfare
 Hotel Administration
 Industrial and Labor Relations
 Public Utilities and
  Transportation
 American Culture
 Recreation Administration

the number of state institutions authorized to prepare students for the doctorate, even though this is not the most critical aspect of the shortage. Two other lines of effort seem likely to be more efficacious. Doctoral study could be made more attractive if it were more efficiently planned so that most students might be assured of reaching their goal within four or five years after the bachelor's degree rather than after seven to twelve years. Suggestions of this kind of acceleration are met by the objection that the degree will then be a "course-work doctorate" instead of an "independent study and research" doctorate, and that the ability to do creative work will not be a part of the requirements. This point is countered by the observation that the present highly unsystematic arrangements do not guarantee that candidates have the skill to carry on research; what they do guarantee, however, is that most of the students will have gone through a long and costly period of uncertainty and frustration. However the graduate experience may be organized, it seems certain that more students would persevere to the final degree if the period of study could be shortened.

The second step in recruiting more students for doctoral programs is financial. Doctoral study at best is a long and expensive course. Since most graduate students are married, they feel obligated to combine work and study. As a result, fatigue increases; the quality of study suffers; and far too many candidates give up, not because of inability to pass the academic hurdles, but because continued effort seems not to be worthwhile. Steps have been taken to increase the amount of financial support for graduate study through generous fellowships, scholarships, and assistantships. In addition, there is need to improve salary levels for young doctoral graduates so that the struggle and the sacrifice of graduate study will seem more rewarding.

Research

Universities at their beginning acted as conservators, accepting and interpreting the knowledge that was available in the culture, but feeling no responsibility to extend the boundaries of that knowledge. Many of the fundamental discoveries of science from the Renaissance to the Industrial Revolution were made by men working independently, without organized projects and without university affiliations. With the growth of the German universities and the spread of their influence to America, and with the development of the concept of graduate study, the two roles of professor and investigator came to be so closely linked that a record of research was made a prerequisite to a university appointment.

At the beginning of this amalgamation, the professor knew that the pursuit of scholarship was his primary obligation. The world was full of unanswered questions, and it was the duty and the joy of the professor to seek answers. He felt no obligation to discover usable, rewarding, or popular answers. He asked only the freedom to seek the truth and to teach it as he understood it. The sequence of *Lernfreiheit* and *Lehrfreiheit* came to be unified in the concept of academic freedom, so that on any campus dedicated men were found seeking to broaden their own understanding along with that of their students. As their studies proceeded, new scholarly disciplines grew up. Deepened understanding exposed more problems to be solved and more old errors to be refuted in every aspect of human concern.

It was not enough, however, for the inquiring professor simply to communicate his discoveries to his own students, so he published his findings. At this point a new pressure of urgency was introduced into the laboratories. Some of the professor's readers perceived applications for the new insights he described, perhaps even profitable applications. They asked him or his students to come out of the library, the study, or the laboratory and explain to them the nature and the meaning of the new knowledge. This step was the beginning of extension service in public institutions, but it was also the beginning of the decline of "pure science." It introduced a relationship between the university and the people that was formalized in the land-grant acts, and that caused in the professor an inner conflict about his role that recently has become acute.

It was pleasant for a while to realize that the results of one's labor were valued by others. The findings of pure research could be applied if they seemed applicable, or ignored if they had no bearing on practical problems. The professor's freedom of choice up to this point was unimpaired. Extension work and the applications of research findings, though, led to sponsored research; and sponsored research has important consequences for freedom of study, for the role of the university in society and the role of the professor in the university, and for the entire nature of the scientific process.

In the beginning, research began with any likely question and accepted any answer, even a negative one. Sponsored research focuses on an answer that will have practical utility. The result becomes more important than the process and excitement of search. Answers and discoveries can be condemned because they are partial, useless to the sponsor, unprofitable, or even in conflict with desired outcomes. Because the sponsorship of research by industry or by government brings funds to the university, faculty members may be diverted from their primary tasks. As a consequence, a major part of the academic work of the university comes to be planned outside the university, usually without full awareness of the effects of the new activity on the primary functions of the university as instructor of youth and free inquirer into the secrets of nature. State institutions, created in part to provide service to their constituents, are especially vulnerable to the incursions of all sorts of sponsored research.

Other undesired results may accompany the increases in sponsored research. The money spent by government and industry for research not only may bring about an imbalance among the basic elements of the faculty, as when physical sciences are overemphasized and humanities neglected, but also may exert pressure on the entire curriculum and educational policy of an institution that has come to depend upon a continuation of these subsidies. As increasing numbers of youth seek the basic elements of higher education, the increase of sponsored research tends to decrease the numbers of professors available for teaching and to dilute their attention to the instructional part of their task.

Still, the concept of the university is changing to include sponsored research, for reasons set forth by Henderson.[10] He suggests that so long as universities have answers, industry will continue to come for assistance; that several industries can join to sponsor university research, although no one of them could afford such a laboratory alone; that government—local, state, and national—has a right to expect research assistance from state universities in national defense as well as in personnel policies, agriculture, public health, engineering, architecture, or any other field; that individuals, such as farmers and small businessmen, cannot do much research by themselves; and that, since a good deal of needed research is not expected to bring an economic reward, the university is best fitted to carry on this sort of study.

University research—pure and applied, sponsored and unsponsored—has contributed beyond measure to the quality of American

---

[10] Algo D. Henderson, *Policies and Practices in Higher Education* (New York: Harper & Row, Publishers, 1960), pp. 149–50.

life; and it will contribute even more as the age of space exploration proceeds, bringing to the door of the university new problems to be solved, new kinds of data to be analyzed, new professions to be taught, and new opportunities to bring the university and its supporting public into closer and more harmonious cooperation.

The Dilemma of Quality and Quantity

If higher percentages of all young people are to go to college, at the same time that their total numbers are increasing most rapidly and at the time when there is a serious shortage of qualified professional staff, how can the quality of education possibly be preserved and enhanced?

If self-selection for college is to continue to be the major factor in determining college attendance, efforts must be expanded to assist each young person to select wisely for himself and for the nation. At present, a small proportion of unfit high school graduates are admitted to state colleges and universities. These students are not the major problem in attaining a high quality of higher education, because within a short period they will be disqualified and leave. More severe threats to quality arise from the high proportions of able youth who do not attend college, either because of lack of desire or lack of funds. An equally distressing fact is that some students, competent and well-prepared, enroll in the wrong college, or in the wrong curriculum, and leave in disillusionment and failure. These considerations point to the desirability of having even more young people enroll and attend for longer periods, thus compounding the problems of quality in the face of quantity.[11]

Quality in public higher education can be safeguarded if several conditions are provided for and safeguarded. First, the diversity of personal traits and ambitions of college-bound youth must be provided for by diversity of courses available in public institutions, all of high quality and of satisfactory prestige, but planned to serve diverse functions. In order to achieve this aim, several of the states already have moved to supplement their state universities by the establishment of locally controlled two-year community colleges. Whatever pattern of organization is adopted, it should provide clear-

---

[11] Educational Policies Commission, *Higher Education in a Decade of Decision* (Washington, D.C.: National Education Association, 1957), Chap. II.

cut descriptions of the objectives of each institution and opportunities for each to perform excellently the tasks assigned to it.

Second, this diversity must be matched by appropriate guidance for youth. In the days of a simple curriculum and few colleges, guidance was unnecessary. Only a single choice—to attend or not to attend—was needed. The complexity of institutional organization that is appearing in American higher education imposes greater strain on the student. Part of the high school guidance effort must be directed toward helping young people understand the varieties of colleges and of curriculums, understand their own qualities and ambitions, and make a choice of colleges and courses in harmony with these understandings. At the same time, the emphasis in the admissions offices of the state institutions can change to one of positive selection of those who seem most likely to profit from attending each college.

Third, each of the institutions within a state pattern of higher education could improve its standards by increased emphasis on the quality of instruction. If curricular diversity is supplemented by improved guidance and buttressed by concern for excellent teaching, it will be possible for state universities and colleges to accommodate greater numbers, and, at the same time, achieve excellence in the pursuit of the appropriate objectives of each curriculum.

CHAPTER IV

Differentiation and Control

The rapid increase in numbers of students enrolling in state-supported colleges and universities implies an increased range of educational backgrounds and educational aspirations among students. To provide for this increasing diversity, new varieties of educational services will be needed. During the past two decades, nearly all the states have studied their emerging needs in higher education and have considered ways of adapting existing institutions and creating new ones to care for them.

During the nineteenth century, diversification beyond that of the university was provided by establishing colleges for varieties of specialized purposes. In general, most of these colleges of limited curriculum have developed into comprehensive institutions. Their history may indicate answers to current questions.

In the coming period of growth, shall some of the new educational services be segregated in newly established colleges or institutes, in order to protect the quality and integrity of established colleges and universities? Shall all institutions, new and established, be expected to provide as broad a spectrum of curriculums as possible? What combination of breadth and specialization seems to be both economically feasible and socially and educationally desirable? What patterns of organization, control, differentiation, and coordination are emerging as the several states prepare for the higher education of their citizens in the years ahead? This chapter examines some of the basic considerations underlying the problem, and presents four examples of state-wide plans for the development and coordination of higher education.

Institutional Specialization

Many of the specialized colleges, the teachers' colleges, and agricultural or technical schools have become multipurpose colleges (see Chapter II). The broadening of the curriculum has gone on in a more or less accidental fashion, without deliberate planning in advance. Before additional campuses are developed to care for the higher education of the coming generations of students, a rational decision should be reached on the question of institutional specialization. If not every college can be expected to become a university and to include a technical school as well, what is the nature of the economical and efficient organization?

The early and traditional approach to the problem of differentiation of function was to establish separate institutions with separate governing boards for each of the newly emerging specializations. In the first half of the nineteenth century, schools of medicine and schools of science, if they were established at all, were separately established. In the second half of that century, normal schools and teachers' colleges, agricultural and mechanical colleges, military schools, and women's colleges were established independently of the state universities. In the South, separate colleges were established for Negroes. In several states, regionally titled colleges and normal schools were set up. At the time, there were reasons for such extensive diversification.

One source of the differentiation of state colleges certainly was political expediency. The multiplication of boards of trustees multiplied the numbers of deserving citizens whose services could be recognized by an appointment that carried much honor and little responsibility. The competing ambitions of growing communities in frontier states also made it seem politically expedient to assign some sort of institution to as many localities as possible.

There are better reasons than the political for the establishment of specialized institutions. The concentration of students and faculty intent on a single curriculum or category of curriculums can lead to a high quality of accomplishment in that field. Even though the early land-grant colleges found it difficult to attract students to agriculture and to find sufficient subject matter to teach them in a four-year course, it is certain that the agricultural colleges that were separated from the faculties and the student bodies of the university had greater freedom to expand their curriculums and to develop scientific approaches to their special subject matter. Within existing universities in all but one or two of the states, the agricultural students and faculties were likely to suffer from low prestige and from unsympathetic policies emanating from the other faculties.

Economy in the provision of technical facilities and of highly qualified faculty members is an additional consideration that argues for specialized institutions. Especially in a sparsely populated state with a meager tax base, in which only a small number of students could be expected to pursue a course in mining, agriculture, or engineering, it is sensible to establish in a single location the expensive instructional land and buildings and equipment, and to gather the students there, rather than to attempt to bring the instruction to the students by duplication of curriculums in all the colleges and universities of the state.

Some of these arguments no longer seem so convincing as they once did. The concentration of attention and effort of faculty and students on a single educational objective now seems unwise, since it is recognized that a graduate should be a cultivated person and a competent citizen as well as a worker. Even from their first beginnings, and increasingly of recent years, the specialized colleges have offered liberal courses as a part of their total graduation requirements. This broader offering then attracts local students who do not desire the specialty, and so it dilutes the unanimity of purpose of faculty and students that was the original justification for the college or institute. Trying to stem the influx of general students, some teachers' colleges for a time required all graduates to earn a teaching certificate even if they never intended to teach, and technological institutes required courses in engineering of students who were uninterested in becoming engineers.

Such requirements reduced the quality of the preparation for the occupations, because they introduced uninterested and often resentful students into the specialized classes. The natural reaction of the faculty was a movement to introduce new curriculums that would be of value to the misplaced students, thus destroying one presumed advantage of institutional concentration of purpose. This is the process through which state colleges in several of the states have become state universities.

As a result of the experiences of the past century with both specialized and comprehensive institutions of higher education, many practical factors now encourage an emphasis on a broader scope of services for each college. Not the least of these factors is the regional character of the enrollment at all American institutions of higher education. The largest and best-known state universities draw many students from all parts of the world and from all over their state, but more than half of their students graduate from high schools within commuting distance of the campus. This local clientele is found in every public college and university. Many of the commuting students, moreover, are enabled to attend any college only because one is conveniently situated near their homes. As stated by Russell: "To a large extent, college attendance is geographically determined. . . . If it is the goal of the state to provide opportunities for higher education to the maximum number of its young people, institutions should be distributed widely." [1] But if the curriculum of the local college is narrowly circumscribed, students will either accept it regardless of its suitability for them or stay away from college. If the curriculum is broad and varied, their chances of being well-educated are enhanced.

Rising numbers of students and the expanding radius of convenient travel assist in the development of comprehensive curriculums. When only four per cent of youth attended college, most state institutions were likely to be so small that they could afford only one or a very few options in undergraduate study. Now that the population concentrates increasingly in urban centers and as many as 32 per cent of college-age youth attend college, the size of institutions justifies the duplication of specialized faculties and equipment in more than one center, at least in the more densely populated states.

The comprehensive college may be justified further, under present economic and social conditions, by the consideration that all men need both breadth and depth in their education and that the occupational and the cultural parts of the curriculum complement each other and lead to the development of a competent and integrated personality. From the standpoint of the student, moreover, the broad curriculum enables him to delay his final choice of educational objective until he has more experience, more judgment, and more awareness of alternatives. If the only available college is specialized, many students have no choice but to attend it; if the available college is broadly diversified, the student may sample several fields of study before making an informed and reasonable selection.

For all the reasons mentioned, it seems probable that state institu-

---

[1] John Dale Russell, *Higher Education in Michigan: The Final Report of the Survey* (Lansing, Mich.: Legislative Study Commission on Higher Education, 1958), p. 8.

tions of higher education will continue their trends toward increasing size of enrollments, with the median size above 1000 students, and toward the breadth and diversity of curriculum made possible by larger enrollments. The differentiation of functions between state-supported institutions within each state, moreover, will be achieved by assigning various periods of attendance or various degree objectives to each college, instead of distributing specialized curriculums among several institutions of limited scope.

Within this sort of horizontal diversification, several cautions must be observed. One is that the college with the shortest term of years (the junior college) must not be considered and must not become an institution of inferior quality. Each state-supported institution of higher education must define its goals clearly and must strive to achieve excellence in achieving each of them. Excellence in education inheres not so much in the quality of the subject matter taught as in the relation of the subject matter to the needs and the purposes of the student and in the thoroughness and rigor in the mastery of the appropriate subject matter.

> Our conception of excellence must embrace many kinds of achievement at many levels. There is no single scale or simple set of categories in terms of which to measure excellence. There is excellence in abstract intellectual activity, in art, in music, in managerial activities, in craftsmanship, in human relations, in technical work. . . . Our society will have passed an important milestone of maturity when those who are the most enthusiastic proponents of a democratic way of life are also the most vigorous proponents of excellence.[2]

A second caution is that students must not be too rigidly assigned to one institution or another on the basis of high school achievement or of scores on college aptitude tests. There is a tendency to assume that the best students should attend the institution with the longest term of years, and that the poorest should be assigned to other, newer, more practical, less well-regarded, or otherwise inferior institutions. Differing minimum qualifications for entrance to the several varieties of higher education are reasonable, but there will still be ex-

---

2 *The Pursuit of Excellence: Education and the Future of America*, Special Studies Report V, Rockefeller Brothers Fund (Garden City, N.Y.: Doubleday & Company, Inc., 1958), pp. 16–17. © 1958 by Rockefeller Brothers Fund, Inc. (as it appears in *Prospect for America*, © 1961). Reprinted by permission of Doubleday & Company, Inc.

tensive overlapping of the distributions of ability. Each institution should have both space and strong curriculums for students of high native ability, and each should afford opportunity for students of good but undistinguished talents to qualify for admission on the basis of proved attainments. College achievement, even at the doctorate level, depends on a combination of ability, opportunity, background, motivation, and character. The state institution that seeks excellence mainly through excessively high and inflexible standards of selection of students may fail to serve its state adequately, and in the process may alienate itself from the understanding and support of the citizens.

Differentiation and Control in Five States

In several states the provision of an appropriate diversification of higher education has been coupled with a regional dispersion of the institutions of higher education. In the regional pattern, universities are placed in one or more sites in the state to provide graduate study and doctoral programs as needed for the state as a whole. In addition, a number of university branches or state colleges, or both, are established throughout the state to bring at least the first years of higher education close to the homes of students. Usually, each of the local campuses of the university or each of the regional colleges combines a general course with occupational specializations needed throughout the state, and they attempt to supplement these two parts of the curriculum with courses of particular interest to the region in which the college is located.

An example of such regional diversification may be found in Pennsylvania. The Pennsylvania State University, established in 1855, is situated at approximately the geographic center of the state, remote from all of the centers of population. On its major campus the University enrolls some 17,000 students and offers all the undergraduate and graduate specializations that are suitable to a major state university. In addition, the University has established 15 Commonwealth Campuses at locations not otherwise served by state-supported institutions of higher education. These Commonwealth Campuses offer two years of study, but they are not uniform in their functions. Enrollments vary from about 500 to more than 4500, and fully 80 per cent of the total enrollment is made up of special part-time students. Some of the campuses offer at present only terminal occupational two-year courses, but most offer a combination of studies paralleling those at the University Park campus plus terminal courses adapted to the industry of the region.

In addition to the Pennsylvania State University with its 15 two-year commonwealth centers, Pennsylvania supports 14 state colleges. These institutions were established as state teachers' colleges between the years of 1857 and 1927. Each has its own governing board of trustees, appointed by the governor for six-year terms, although educational policy for the state colleges since 1949 has been legally assigned to the Board of Presidents of State Colleges. The colleges have expanded their original function of teacher preparation to include liberal arts training and occupational specialization as needed in their regions. Students from any part of the state may attend any of the regional state colleges, or the University, if they are qualified for admission. In Pennsylvania, some opportunity for state-supported higher education is within geographic range of almost every high school graduate. Nevertheless, fewer than 0.4 per cent of the total population were enrolled for degree-credit in public institutions of higher education in 1960. This figure compares with proportions at least four times as large in Michigan (1.6), Kansas (1.9), Minnesota (1.6), Oklahoma (1.9) and Washington (1.8). In the same year, Massachusetts had slightly more than 0.5 per cent of its total population in degree-credit enrollment in public higher education; New York, 0.7 per cent; and California, 2.4 per cent.[3] These samplings of the experience of nine of the more populous states indicate that regional dispersion of institutions does not by itself provide a high level of effective educational opportunity.

Institutional diversification. The State of Michigan in the past has provided for differentiation of collegiate opportunity by establishing a series of autonomous institutions. The three major state-controlled universities are governed by separate boards created by authority of the State Constitution and elected by popular vote. The College of Mining and Technology, Ferris Institute, and Grand Valley College were created by legislative enactment; their boards

---

[3] Enrollments from Table 18, *Opening (Fall) Enrollment in Higher Education, 1960: Analytic Report* (Washington, D.C.: Government Printing Office, 1961), p. 23. Population figures from April, 1960, census, as reported in *Health, Education and Welfare Trends,* 1961 ed. (Washington, D.C.: Government Printing Office, 1961), p. 109.

are appointed by the governor with the advice and consent of the senate. The four regional institutions are governed by the constitutionally established State Board of Education, which has elected membership. The State Board also has responsibility for approval of local community colleges. It has supervision over their institutional boards in the same way as over other school district boards. The history of specialized institutions in Michigan exhibits once more the trend for four-year colleges and universities to move toward a comprehensive liberal curriculum in addition to their original specialized purposes.

One of the major recommendations of a 1958 survey of higher education in Michigan [4] was that more effective coordination of the state-controlled program of higher education be provided through the creation of a state Coordinating Board. The survey reported:

> Little or nothing has been done to coordinate the total program of publicly controlled and privately controlled higher education in Michigan. There are some voluntary associations that meet annually for the discussion of common problems, but these are relatively weak and ineffective in Michigan. Even the communication among institutions, and particularly between the publicly controlled and the privately controlled groups, has not been good in Michigan. . . . In summary, it must be concluded that coordination of institutional programs of higher education in Michigan is almost non-existent. Each of the publicly controlled institutions operates completely independently of all the others, except in the case of the four that are under the State Board of Education. Even among these four the coordination is limited to such matters as a geographical or territorial designation of responsibility and a supposedly uniform salary scale. The pattern of control through boards for the State-controlled institutions is rather confused, and no consistent plan has been followed in setting up the boards for the various publicly controlled institutions of higher education in the state.[5]

In the light of this need, the Director of the Survey recommended separate, appointed, constitutionally established boards for each of the state-supported four-year colleges, plus the creation of a Coordinating Board, eventually to have constitutional status and authority commensurate with its responsibilities and with the status of the universities it was to coordinate. The Coordinating Board would

---

[4] John Dale Russell, *op. cit.*
[5] *Ibid.*, p. 110–11.

be assigned six major functions by statute, and would in like fashion be specifically excluded from authority over the internal administration of any of the institutions.

The functions recommended for the Michigan Coordinating Board were detailed as follows:

> One of the important functions of the Coordinating Board would be the collection, analysis, and reporting of data concerning the programs, facilities, finances, and operations of all the State-controlled institutions of higher education. The Coordinating Board should be the agency through which the Legislature and all other State agencies are furnished whatever information they need about the institutions of higher education. . . .
>
> A second function of the Coordinating Board would be to furnish the State fiscal authorities and the Legislature an annual estimate of the needs of each State-controlled institution for appropriations for the coming fiscal year. . . .
>
> A third function of the Coordinating Board would be to advise the Legislature and other agencies of State Government on all policy matters affecting the development and operation of higher education in the State. . . .
>
> A fourth function of the Coordinating Board would be to make continuing studies of the State's need for higher education, and of the effectiveness of the programs presently maintained by the institutions. . . .
>
> A fifth function of the Coordinating Board would be to provide a source, through its staff, from which the officials of the institutions in the State could obtain wise advice and counsel on the problems of developing and operating their programs. . . .
>
> Finally, the Coordinating Board should be given authority to make such test checks and audits of institutional records as it deems necessary to insure the accuracy and uniformity of the reports that are made to it.[6]

In 1959 a bill was introduced in the Michigan Legislature to establish a Commission on Higher Education to review and make recommendations on budgets and to make continuing studies of financial needs, programs, and degree offerings of state-supported colleges and universities. Again, in 1961 a bill was proposed that would establish a State Council on Higher Education to promote the development and maintenance of a coordinated state system of higher education. Neither bill was enacted.

---

[6] *Ibid.*, p. 115–16.

Curricular specialization. North Carolina provides geographical dispersion of its colleges as well as differentiation by curricular specialization. The Consolidated University includes a separate State College of Agriculture and Engineering and a separate Woman's College. Nine state colleges and state teachers' colleges are separately established and governed; the student body at five of these is predominantly Negro.

North Carolina has also provided for the autonomous governance of its institutions of higher education, with ten separate boards responsible for 12 four-year colleges. The Board of Trustees of the University of North Carolina governs and coordinates the three institutional units of the University: the University of North Carolina, Chapel Hill; the University of North Carolina State College, Raleigh; and the University of North Carolina Woman's College, Greensboro. In addition, separate board of trustees are established for each of the following colleges: (1) Agricultural and Technical College of North Carolina, Greensboro; (2) Appalachian State Teachers College, Boone; (3) Elizabeth City State Teachers College; (4) Fayetteville State Teachers College; (5) North Carolina College, Durham; (6) Pembroke State College; (7) East Carolina College, Greenville; (8) Western Carolina College, Cullowhee; (9) Winston-Salem Teachers College.

The five junior colleges in North Carolina (1962) are governed by local boards appointed in part by the governor, although a majority of the members are appointed by local authorities, and all must be residents of the local area or at least of counties contiguous to the location of the junior college. In all other respects except the governor's participation in formation of the board, the governance and the support of these five junior colleges has been similar to those in other states; and the institutions are primarily local rather than state institutions of higher education.

The activities of all 17 public institutions of higher education (including the five locally controlled junior colleges) are coordinated by the North Carolina Board of Higher Education. The purpose of the Board has been "to plan and promote the development of a sound, vigorous, progressive, and coordinated system of higher education in the State." As summarized by Martorana and Hollis:

> In pursuit of this objective the board will seek the cooperation of all the institutions of higher education and of other educational

agencies in planning a system of higher education that will serve all the higher educational needs of the State and that will encourage a high standard of excellence in all institutions composing the system, each operating under the direction of its own board of trustees in the performance of the functions assigned to it. The board shall allot the major functions and activities of each of the State institutions in keeping with the purposes for which the institution was established; determine the types of degrees to be awarded by each of the institutions; prescribe uniform statistical reporting practices for all of the State's institutions; and review and appraise the biennial budget requests for all institutions.[7]

In August, 1962, the Governor's Commission on Education Beyond the High School recommended a reconstitution of the Board of Higher Education that would include on the Board four presidents of public institutions of higher learning; emphasize the planning and coordination functions of the Board; strengthen the budgetary and advisory powers of the Board; and make it clear that comprehensive community colleges are under the jurisdiction of the State Board of Education, rather than the Board of Higher Education.

In another section, the *Report* recommended that three of the five public junior colleges be converted to nonresidential public senior colleges, each with its own board of trustees. The *Report* further recommended the establishment of one system of fifteen public, two-year, post-high school institutions offering college-parallel, technical-vocational-terminal, and adult education instruction tailored to area needs. A plan was also presented for the governance of these institutions by local boards and their supervision by the State Board of Education.[8]

Institutional variety under a single governing board. In Kansas, three varieties of state institutions of higher education provide for differentiation of senior college opportunities. The five state institutions are supplemented by 14 locally controlled public junior colleges, each governed by a local school board and operated under the general supervision of the State Board of Education and its executive officer, the State Superintendent of Public Instruction.

---

[7] S. V. Martorana and Ernest V. Hollis, *State Boards Responsible for Higher Education,* Office of Education Circular No. 619 (Washington, D.C.: Government Printing Office, 1960), p. 129.

[8] *The Report of the Governor's Commission on Education Beyond the High School* (Raleigh, N.C.: The Commission, 1962).

The state four-year colleges and universities are controlled by a single governing and coordinating board, The State Board of Regents. This bipartisan board of nine members is responsible for five institutions: (1) University of Kansas, Lawrence; (2) Kansas State University of Agriculture and Applied Science, Manhattan; (3) Fort Hays Kansas State College; (4) Kansas State Teachers College, Emporia; (5) Kansas State College of Pittsburg. The State Board of Regents controls budgets, programs, personnel policies, and the planning and financing of plant for all five institutions. All state-supported and controlled higher education in Kansas is included under the governance of the Regents.[9]

A tripartite master plan.   Faced with a projected doubling of college enrollments within a decade, the California Legislature in 1959 asked the University-State College Liaison Committee "to prepare a Master Plan for the development, expansion, and integration of the facilities, curriculum, and standards of higher education of the State, to meet the needs of the State during the next ten years and thereafter." The Master Plan was submitted, as directed, at the 1960 session of the legislature, and the major features of the plan were enacted into law at that session.

At the time of the preparation of the Master Plan, publicly supported higher education in California included 63 public junior colleges, offering at least two years (but less than four years) of college-level studies beyond the twelfth grade, locally governed, financed partly by the state and partly by the local school district, and subject to supervision by the State Department of Education. Legally, these junior colleges were part of the public school system and were classified as secondary schools. They are not, within the definition adopted for this volume, state institutions, but they are a part of the differentiated pattern of higher education in California, and were of concern to the Master Plan Survey Team. The second part of the tripartite system at the time of the survey consisted of 13 state colleges, offering work through the master's degree in several fields, supported directly from state funds for both current costs and capital outlays, and governed by the State Board of Education. The third segment was the University of California. It included seven

---

[9] *Kansas Plans for the Next Generation,* a report on higher education in Kansas to the Board of Regents by a panel of advisors (Topeka, Kan.: Board of Regents, 1962), pp. 6–13.

campuses in 1959, governed by the Regents of the University of California (a constitutionally autonomous corporation), and was supported by State funds. Although the University is a single entity, each of its campuses enjoys a considerable degree of autonomy. In 1959, there were two university campuses with enrollments in excess of 16,000 (at Berkeley and at Los Angeles); the College of Medicine in San Francisco; and four liberal arts campuses, each with enrollments under 3000.[10]

Faced with this complex of institutions and organizational patterns, the Master Plan Survey Team set itself two major objectives for the plan it would develop. First, the Master Plan "must guard the state and state funds against unwarranted expansion and unhealthy competition among the segments of public higher education. Second, it must provide abundant collegiate opportunities for qualified young people and give the segments and institutions enough freedom to furnish the diverse higher educational services needed by the state."[11]

The Master Plan Survey Team studied questions of structure, function, and coordination; quantity and quality in students; institutional capacities and regional needs; faculty demand and supply; adult education; costs; and California's ability to finance higher education. For the present discussion, the action of the legislature on the definition of function for each of the three segments, and the establishment of the coordinating council, are the elements of primary concern.

The Donahoe Higher Education Act[12] opens with general provisions that establish important fundamental principles. One is a definition: "Public higher education consists of (1) all public junior colleges heretofore and hereafter established pursuant to law, (2) all state colleges heretofore and hereafter established pursuant to law, and (3) each campus, branch and function of the University of California heretofore and hereafter established by the Regents of the University of California."[13] Two aspects of the definition are

---

[10] Since 1959, there have been new establishments of six junior colleges and two state colleges. The University of California is building (1962) two additional new campuses and is planning for two others.

[11] *A Master Plan for Higher Education in California, 1960–1975* (Sacramento, Calif.: California State Department of Education, 1960), p. 27.

[12] *California Education Code*, Division 16.5, "Higher Education." The Act is reproduced in full in *A Master Plan, op. cit.*, pp. 199–203.

[13] *California Education Code*, Section 22500.

noteworthy. First, the junior colleges are legally recognized as a part of higher education, even though later Section 22650 provides that they shall also "continue to be a part of the public school system of this State." Second, the definition clearly differentiates between the establishment *pursuant to law* of the junior colleges and state colleges, and the establishment *by the Regents* of "each campus, branch and function" of the University.

The policy statement of the Act is an integral part of the entire concept of a tripartite system. It is unusual as a subject for legislation, but its importance as a guideline for the institutions, their governing boards, the public, and the students cannot be overestimated: "Each segment of public higher education shall strive for excellence in its sphere, as assigned in this division." [14]

The University of California is declared to be the primary state-supported academic agency for research. It may provide instruction in the liberal arts and sciences and in the professions; it has exclusive jurisdiction in public higher education over instruction in the profession of law and over graduate instruction in the professions of medicine, dentistry, veterinary medicine, and architecture. It has the sole authority in public higher education to award the doctoral degree in all fields of learning, except that it may agree on joint doctoral programs with the state colleges.

In dealing with the state colleges, the problem of the Donahoe Act was not to protect existing rights and status, but rather to establish conditions that would permit the colleges to achieve a recognized and respected share in the total work of higher education. A separate State College Board of Trustees was established, but as a creation by the Legislature rather than as a constitutional body; the Board lacks the almost complete independence from legislative control enjoyed by the Regents of the University. In the definition of their functions, the state colleges share some of the responsibilities of the university and some of those assigned mainly to the junior colleges.

Liberal education is emphasized, but professional education is limited to the masters' degree, with emphasis primarily on practical and applied fields. Research is authorized, so long as it does not interfere with the primary function of instruction; graduate study

---

[14] *Ibid.*, Section 22502.

beyond the master's degree may be developed jointly with the University, if the University wishes to cooperate in this endeavor.

The major effect of the Donahoe Act upon the junior colleges lay in their explicit inclusion as a part of public higher education in California. No new administrative arrangements were developed, and no new functions were assigned. The junior colleges remain a part of the public school system, subject to the minimum standards and general supervision of the State Board of Education. They shall "offer instruction through but not beyond the fourteenth grade level, which instruction may include, but shall not be limited to, programs in one or more of the following categories: (1) standard collegiate courses for transfer to higher institutions; (2) vocational and technical fields leading to employment; and (3) general or liberal arts courses. Studies in these fields may lead to the associate in arts or associate in science degree." [15]

The California Master Plan for Higher Education, in summary, provides for availability of three kinds of higher education in all populous areas of the state. All are instructed to seek excellence in each program that is offered; all share in a responsibility for general liberal education; all are expected to provide equivalent courses at the freshman and sophomore level to prepare students for upper division baccalaureate study. To this extent, all institutions serve students of similar ambitions and aptitudes—students who make their choice of college not on the basis of their own academic purposes, but rather for reasons of cost, proximity, peer influences, family tradition, putative prestige, or social advantages.

The three levels of institution, though widely available in a geographic sense, are sharply diversified in their specialized purposes. The junior colleges are the only institutions authorized to offer two-year occupational courses for students who do not intend at the time of enrollment to seek a bachelor's degree. The fields of specialization for the state colleges include undergraduate preprofessional curriculums and occupational preparation at the four- or five-year level for practical fields such as teaching, business administration, engineering, social work, and criminology. The university specializes in advanced studies and in research; professional preparation is explicitly reserved to it.

---

[15] *Ibid.*, Section 22651.

As a consequence of this diversification by level, it is expected that four-fifths of the freshmen and sophomores of the state will be enrolled in the junior colleges, that the state colleges will have a greater number of upper division students than lower division students, and that the graduate enrollments at the Berkeley and Los Angeles campuses will exceed those of any of the undergraduate classes.

From the standpoint of the student, the plan assures that self-selection for higher education can be preserved in California. No high school graduate will be denied an opportunity to attempt, at the junior college, to qualify for further study; and every qualified student will find public higher education as far as or beyond the doctorate available at several locations within the state.

Because of the complexity and size of the higher education establishment, coordination is provided through a Coordinating Council that is advisory to the governing boards of the institutions of higher education and to appropriate state officials. The Council reviews the budget requests of the institutions, makes recommendations to the governor and to the legislature for changes in the functions and programs of the segments of higher education, and recommends plans for orderly growth of higher education and for the location of new facilities and programs. It can require institutions to submit data on costs, selection and retention of students, enrollments, plant capacities, and other matters pertinent to effective planning and coordination; and it must report to the governor and legislature as requested. The coordinating authority is left in the hands of the governor and the legislature; the Council's importance inheres in the fact that it studies the problems of higher education and makes its recommendations to the governor and the legislature.

Summary

The descriptions of provision for diversity of educational opportunity in five states illustrate several of the key issues of diversity and coordination that are being solved by each state in the light of its own existing structure, history, predicted future, and political heritage. A basic issue is the degree of autonomy of institutions. Shall it be achieved through constitutionally established boards for each institution as in Michigan, or shall it be limited by establishing single boards for groups of similar institutions as in California, or by establishing a single board for all state higher education as in Kansas? The need for coordination is evident under each system, but the nature and power of the coordinating board are still at issue. The voluntary board in Michigan and the purely advisory board in North Carolina are criticized within their own states as being ineffective; yet in both states cautions are voiced against granting a coordinating board power to control internal operation of any college or university.

The autonomy guaranteed by constitutional establishment of the corporate structure of a board is valued in Michigan, California, and North Carolina. The statutory establishment of governing boards in Pennsylvania, Kansas, and in the California State Colleges is seen as a threat to autonomy, in that legislative change may be both swifter and more politically inspired than constitutional amendments. The need for the geographical dispersion of colleges throughout the State is recognized in each state; the issue revolves about the kind and the extent of specialization of the several regional establishments. In the states sampled in this chapter, the trend is toward the establishment of broad educational opportunities in each state-supported institution of higher education.

CHAPTER V

The Federal Government
and Higher Education

Although the federal government has not established a national university, it would be a mistake to assume that it has no interest in higher education and is not concerned with state colleges and universities. As a matter of fact, the federal government was never so involved in American higher education as it is today. Since World War II an entirely new dimension has been added; most American colleges and universities—private and public, large and small, church-related and independent—are now participating in some federal program, grant, or subsidy that aids either the institution directly, its faculty, or its students. The extent of these involvements is generally unknown, even by the administrators concerned. A symposium, "The Federal Government and Higher Education," revealed widespread misunderstanding on the part of the participants, presumably the leaders of American higher education.[1]

Moreover, it is doubtful that an adequate description of the extent of the present participation of the federal government in higher education would have much validity in a few years, or even in a few months. In recent times great advances have been made on several fronts; the federal government is assuming many new roles in such areas as research, student aid, capital improvements, and educational programs of various sorts, including international education. For the first time, there is a growing recognition that national purposes and educational values and programs must more nearly coincide. As a result, every month sees some new proposal in the realm of higher education which represents another challenge to the national traditions with respect to the role of higher education, and more especially to the concept of higher education as a function and responsibility of the several states.

[1] American Assembly, *The Federal Government and Higher Education* (Englewood Cliffs, N.J.: Prentice-Hall, Inc., 1960).

It is now estimated that at least 1600 of the American colleges and universities, public and private, directly participate in one or more of the federal programs of higher education. The 400 which do not are primarily theological schools and small undergraduate and junior colleges.[2] Only a few federal programs to date have involved a wide participation by the colleges. For example, most of the institutions are excluded from the more lucrative research grants, which chiefly go to the recognized graduate schools. Nevertheless, for the citizen indoctrinated in the traditional view that public higher education is a state function only, knowledge of the widespread federal participation may be startling.

A listing of federal programs affecting higher education indicates the extent of present federal involvement with colleges and universities.[3] By departments and independent agencies, the report lists the following numbers of separate agencies with programs that affect institutions of higher education.

Department of Agriculture	6
Department of Commerce	7
Department of Defense	18
Department of Health, Education, and Welfare	50
Department of the Interior	10
Department of Justice	1
Department of Labor	1
Post Office Department	2
Department of State	8
Department of the Treasury	2
Atomic Energy Commission	8
Civil Service Commission	2
Federal Aviation Agency	1
Federal Deposit Insurance Corporation	1
General Service Administration	1
Housing and Home Finance Agency	4
Library of Congress	1
National Aeronautics and Space Administration	1
National Science Foundation	8
Office of Emergency Planning	1
Small Business Administration	1
Smithsonian Institution	4
Tennessee Valley Authority	6
United States Information Agency	1
Veterans Administration	2
International Organizations	20
	167

[2] Nathan M. Pusey, *Harvard and the Federal Government* (Cambridge, Mass.: Harvard University Press, 1961), pp. 1–4.

[3] Frederic Sudermann, *Federal Programs Affecting Higher Education* (Iowa City, Iowa: Division of Special Services, State University of Iowa, 1962). Distributed by American Council on Education, Washington, D.C.

Since some of the 167 agencies offer several varieties of research programs and training plans, the total number of separate federal contracts that could conceivably be executed by a major state university exceeds 200. Because of the extent of the involvement, there is a tendency in certain circles to speak of federal aid for higher education as though there is a recognizable program that reaches all aspects of higher education in all public institutions. Such is not the case. The federal involvement can best be described as a vast array of uncoordinated relationships, each designed to obtain a specific objective of some agency of the federal government. To date, no agency has a congressional mandate to provide general support for higher education.

The segmented federal grants have not been unmixed blessings. They have resulted in pronounced imbalances in the curriculum, having been largely concentrated in the natural sciences, engineering, and medicine. Since federally sponsored programs ordinarily require considerable outlays of space and facilities, the recipients have often provided laboratories when their great need has been for libraries or other facilities that would be of greater benefit to the majority of their students. In fact, at times administrators have wondered if the institutions were not aiding the federal government more than the federal government was aiding the colleges and universities. Nevertheless, so much of enduring value has been contributed to higher education as a whole that it is almost a foregone conclusion that federal participation will continue to grow, and that eventually federal subsidies will be provided for the whole program of higher education.

Although most federal involvement has come in the last two decades, there is a long story of federal relationships to higher education. The first six presidents of the United States recognized the responsibility of the federal government to provide for higher education. President Madison proposed a national university in four annual messages, suggesting seminaries in each state "instituted by the National Legislature, the expense of which might be defrayed out of the vacant grounds which have accrued to the nation within [the states]." [4] This was finally implemented over a hundred

---

[4] Richard Hofstadter and Wilson Smith, *American Higher Education: A Documentary History* (Chicago: University of Chicago Press, 1961), p. 177.

years ago when the Morrill Act of 1862 provided for the land-grant colleges.

Since 1944 there has been a tremendous growth in federal programs related to and in support of higher education. It is impossible to treat here all these programs, but some mention will be made of developments in five areas: programs of education and training, programs of student financial assistance, research programs, programs of international education, and loans and grants for capital outlay.

Federal Programs of Education and Training

In recent years the federal government has embarked upon almost revolutionary practices in order to increase the number and quality of persons with technical, scientific, engineering, and other professional training. Today, practically all federal departments and agencies are involved in educational programs, many of which also involve colleges and universities. Most of these programs, however, are not designed particularly to assist the institutions of higher learning and, consequently, may not be regarded as federal aid programs. Rather, these programs in the main are directed toward the accomplishment of governmental objectives in various areas. Throughout, there can be detected some common American goals, but the programs are specifically directed to the education of specialists in certain professions or of the employees of federal departments and agencies.

The pattern of federal-institutional cooperation evolved out of practices developed during war periods. When specialized personnel were needed for military and defense-related activities, it was quite natural to turn to the colleges and universities. Moreover, enrollments in the colleges in war times were greatly reduced, and space and facilities were available. Without too much alteration, many of these facilities could be used in the government educational programs. Consequently, a procedure for contracting for the needed educational and research facilities was improvised.

After World War II the servicemen returned to college under the veterans' educational benefit legislation. This arrangement also provided precedent for the extension of such arrangements to other types of federal programs and purposes. The G.I. Bill permitted privately controlled institutions, as well as the publicly controlled institutions, to participate in the benefits. Ever since, any college or university has been permitted to apply for consideration in the location of certain government sponsored educational programs. The facilities, resources, and location of the educational institution are the determinants in the selective process.

A major step in the evolution of these programs was the National Defense Education Act of 1958. This act clearly defined the federal interest in higher education. While capitalizing upon previous experience, it evolved contractual and grant procedures that enabled the government to broaden and strengthen the nation's resources in graduate education, to increase the supply of teachers, and to stimulate college attendance through the medium of student loans.

On the whole, however, the programs are still operated under policies and procedures established by the governmental agencies. The federal departments and agencies report to different committees of Congress and operate under differing legislative and executive directives. Within predetermined limits, each of the colleges and universities makes its own policies and forms its own relationships with each separate federal department and agency. It is misleading to speak in this context of "federal government" and "higher education." The institutions of higher learning and the departments and agencies of government are more or less free agents, and each set of units operates plurally. There is no single policy and no single coordinating mechanism. This arrangement preserves the diversity of practices within the institutions of higher learning and the individuality of a given school. Also, it prevents centralized authority in education, but it does cause bureaucracy and involved procedures. The federal programs of fellowships and traineeships are difficult to classify. Although the recipients of the federal funds are individuals, the programs are frequently tailor-made and carry a cost-of-education grant to the institution. The primary purpose of grants for education and training is to provide trained manpower in designated fields needed by the government. For example, through research contracts the government stimulates the solution of problems in given areas, and the benefit to the individual research assistant is incidental. In this sense, research contracts constitute educational programs, but the programs are individualized.

In a brief sketch, it is impossible to explore all the programs in which a federal agency or department makes a formal arrangement with a college or university for the performance of a specialized educational service determined by the federal agency or department. In addition, the federal programs are dynamic and subject to change at any time. The emphasis in the early 1960's, dictated by the cold war, is centered in scientific training. As a result of the federal activity, the science instruction in colleges and universities has improved, and this general improvement has filtered down into the high schools and elementary schools.

In 1959, more than 450 colleges and universities participated in one or more federally sponsored programs. The National Science Foundation reached the largest number, more than 385, both in undergraduate and graduate schools. The National Institutes of Health reached 150, and the Office of Education reached nearly 125.[5]

In these programs of education and training most of the federal money is expended in relatively few colleges and universities. In fact, in 1959, about 84 per cent of the federal funds were allocated to a total of 101 colleges and universities. The agricultural programs are limited to the land-grant colleges. The Public Health funds went to the 85 to 90 universities with schools of medicine or public health. Other grants tended to be concentrated in the 175 universities that confer the Ph.D. degree. Among the undergraduate colleges, more private than public institutions participated, 170 of the former as contrasted to 90 of the latter. These are the strong, well-recognized institutions from which large quotas of graduates continue into graduate and professional schools.

Federal Student Aid in Higher Education

Of recent years there has been considerable federal effort in the field of aid to students. The *Directory of Federally Financed Student Loans, Fellowships and Career Training Programs in the Field of*

---

[5] J. Kenneth Little, *A Survey of Federal Programs in Higher Education—Summary,* Office of Education Bulletin 1963, No. 5 (Washington, D.C.: Government Printing Office, 1962), p. 13.

Higher Education (1962) [6] listed over 300 government programs which provide financial aid to students, either directly or as a consequence of other grants.

Student aid is an important complement to the total national effort to provide higher education for all qualified youth. A high percentage of the most competent high school graduates do not enter college in the United States; many of those who do not attend college would like to do so but feel they cannot afford the costs. Moreover, many of the students who drop out do so for financial reasons, and many work full-time while in school. Consequently, student financial aid is a matter of importance not only to those students who must depend on it if they are to continue their education, but to the nation as well, since trained intelligence is the foundation of national well-being.

Although some scholarships have long been provided by generous donors, federal programs of financial aid are of comparatively recent origin. The federal government entered the field during the period 1935–43, when the National Youth Administration helped keep more than 600,000 American youth in college. World War II brought student loan programs for juniors and seniors and for graduate and professional students in science, engineering, or health programs. During two war years over 11,000 students borrowed $500 per year from the government and agreed to work in the war effort after graduation. After the war, the Serviceman's Readjustment Act (G.I. Bill) and the companion bill for the disabled veterans (P.L. 16) returned hundreds of thousands of American youth to their studies and induced other hundreds of thousands to attend college.

Although by 1959–60 the veterans' programs had shrunk to 50,000 as compared to the 1,235,000 in attendance in 1947–48, a rapidly expanding War Orphans Scholarship Program was developing. In fact, in 1959–60 almost 17 per cent of Veterans Administration education expenditures were for orphans. Finally, over 40,000 students were attending college in 1961, mostly at the graduate level, on research subsidies of one kind or another.

---

[6] U.S. House of Representatives, Committee on Education and Labor, 89th Cong., 2d sess., *A Directory of Federally Financed Student Loans, Fellowships and Career Training Programs in the Field of Higher Education* (Washington, D.C.: Government Printing Office, 1962).

There can be no question that the federal government is interested in having students in colleges and universities. No doubt, much of the current activity is intended to replace in some measure the numerous subventions veterans were receiving immediately following World War II and the Korean episode. Under the G.I. Bill, at one time about 50 per cent of the student population was on government subsidy. At present, no more than five per cent of the student body participates in the National Defense Education Act loan program. Under this act of 1958, the total available federal student loan funds per undergraduate are not yet as high as the funds that were granted during 1955–56.

There are some other interesting aspects to these recent developments in federal assistance to students. For example, the majority of the funds are administered by the institutions at the expense of the institution (which may prove intolerable when the time comes to collect the loans). Apparently, the government has concluded that undergraduate education should be paid for by the student who receives the benefit, but that graduate study should be relatively free to the student. If, however, it is important to recruit more graduate students, it might be advisable to select and subsidize them at the undergraduate level. Again, it is apparent that there is no single national program of student aid; rather, there are numerous programs, each designed to meet a specific purpose of a federal agency. The institutions of higher learning must keep abreast of the intricacies of several hundred programs involving student assistance, at least thirty of which are of major importance. Most of the funds involved are controlled by institutions, and many include a provision for supplementary aid to the institutions attended by aided students. Aids to students are a significant part of the total federal involvement in higher education.

The Federal Research Effort in Higher Education

The increase in federal funds for research since 1940 has been astonishing. The times have demanded research; the nation has been caught up in a scientific and technological age; and a major portion of the responsibility for research has been assigned to the universities. The sums involved are so large as to be unintelligible to the layman. In the decade from 1951 to 1961, the government, industries, colleges, universities, and a variety of nonacademic, nonprofit research agencies spent an aggregate of $80,000,000,000 for research and development activities, not all of it through higher education. As a basis for comparison, it may be noted that this amount was almost exactly comparable to the entire federal budget in the single fiscal year 1961.

The trend of growth can be demonstrated also by a review of only 25 years. In the late 1930's the federal government was budgeting annually less than $1,000,000 for all its programs of research and development. In 1950 the figure was $1,100,000,000; in 1960 it was $8,100,000,000; in 1961 it had risen to $9,200,000,000; and, for 1963, it was estimated that the government would spend $12,-400,000,000 for these purposes.[7]

Of these amounts, about one-fourth are expended for the support of basic and applied research, and the remaining three-fourths go to developmental activities. Only 11 per cent of the over-all federal spending for research and development in the fiscal year 1961 went to institutions of higher learning. Even this proportion represented a great deal of money, especially by traditional standards—about $964,000,000. The estimate for 1962 was $1,200,-000,000.[8]

In order to get the true picture, it must be noted that the figures include the huge amounts of money used to support the great federal research centers under the administration of universities, such as the Argonne National Laboratory of the University of Chicago (including the International Institute of Nuclear Science and Engineering, a pioneering effort in "atoms for peace" training), the Los Alamos Scientific Laboratory supervised by the University of California, and the Applied Physics Laboratory of Johns Hopkins University. In 1961, $401,000,000, over 40 per cent of the total federal expenditure for research and development in institutions of higher learning, were devoted to the maintenance of such federal contract research centers. The balance, $563,000,000, in 1961 went as direct grants to colleges and universities. For 1962 the direct grants were estimated at $732,000,000.

---

[7] John C. Weaver, "The Federal Research Endeavor and Higher Education," in *Higher Education and the Federal Government,* ed. Charles G. Dobbins (Washington, D.C.: American Council on Education, 1963), p. 58.
[8] *Ibid.,* p. 59.

Most of the federal research expenditures, 71 per cent, go to projects in the physical sciences (including mathematics and engineering); 26 per cent, in the life sciences (biological, medical, and agricultural); two per cent, in psychological sciences; and one per cent, to the social studies. The humanities are left with nothing. Medicine has progressed with grants from the United States Public Health Service. Engineering has made great strides in research with contracts and grants from the Department of Defense, the Atomic Energy Commission, and the National Aeronautics and Space Administration. Agriculture, although it provided a smaller part of the gross national product than it did in the earlier agricultural economy, still gets a sizeable amount of government support, even though no more than one-fourth to one-third of the research expenditures of all land-grant institutions comes from the Department of Agriculture.[9]

Of the 2000 colleges and universities in the United States, fewer than 500 receive any federally sponsored research money. In fact, in 1961 more than two-thirds of all the federal research funds were received by twenty-five institutions; four-fifths of the total funds, by fifty schools; and 95 per cent, by one hundred colleges and universities.

The great bulk of the federal research grants to academic organizations goes to three groupings of institutions. These are, respectively, a group of strong private institutions in southern New England and the Mid-Atlantic seaboard, a cluster of large state universities in the Middle West, and a few highly developed private and public institutions on the Pacific Coast.

Certainly it is necessary for federal agencies to place research contracts with organizations having the highest competence to carry through the projects to successful completion. That there are so few universities with this demonstrated competence is not primarily the responsibility of federal agencies. Their responsibility for vital research leads them to place contracts with institutions of well-known and highly developed research potential. In spite of the clamor of lesser institutions for more attention and more money, it is increasingly difficult for them to get into this chosen circle; and, as the chosen institutions improve their services and facilities with the addi-

---

[9] *Ibid.*, p. 61.

tional monies from governmental sources, it is unlikely that they will be overtaken without concerted effort. The remedy lies with the lesser institutions: Let them employ numbers of research scholars and provide for them great libraries and extensive laboratories, and opportunities to obtain research contracts will multiply.

The favored institutions are the primary centers for graduate work and confer most of the doctoral degrees, especially in the subsidized fields. Here, too, are to be found the postdoctoral fellows who can do the desired research under competent supervision. The subsidized fields of study are also likely to become strongly entrenched here, thus attracting more than their traditional or proportionate share of graduate students and candidates for degrees. Also, because of the emphasis on research, as contrasted to the preparation for college teaching, and because of the contrast between research salaries and teaching salaries, these institutions may prepare fewer teachers than will be needed in the years ahead.

Late in 1962 the Carnegie Foundation released *The Carnegie Study of the Federal Government and Higher Education,* based on self-studies conducted by 26 cooperating institutions of higher learning.[10] The 26 institutions were chosen to be fairly representative in size, kind, and location. Together, they received 28 per cent of all government money spent in institutions of higher learning in 1959–60.

The institutions fell into four main categories. The first category consisted of twelve universities with large commitments to research: University of Michigan, Massachusetts Institute of Technology, Stanford University, Harvard University, University of Chicago, University of California at Berkeley, University of Texas, University of California at Los Angeles, Cornell University, Princeton University, University of California at San Diego, and the California Institute of Technology. The amounts varied from $20,000,000 at the University of Michigan to $5,000,000 at the California Institute of Technology.

The second category included institutions receiving from $1.5 million to $3.5 million in federal grants for project research: Pennsylvania State University, Indiana University, Syracuse University, Tulane University, Iowa State University, and University of Cali-

---

[10] Nathan M. Pusey, "The Carnegie Study of the Federal Government and Higher Education," in Charles G. Dobbins, *op. cit.,* pp. 17–29.

fornia at Davis. The third category included four schools receiving $100,000 to $1.5 million, in descending order: University of Louisville, Notre Dame University, Union University, and University of Wyoming. Finally, the Carnegie Study included four institutions—an engineering college, a teacher's college, and two liberal arts colleges—that were relatively uninvolved in federal programs.

The concentration of federal research support in a few institutions is significant to the student who wishes to understand American higher education. The vast majority of the nation's colleges and universities have practically no share in federal research programs. Schools of law, business, public administration, and other graduate and professional schools, as well as colleges and divisions of arts and letters, are almost untouched by this large flow of federal research money. Congress appropriates research funds in the expectation of demonstrable results in national health, defense, or economic development; and it is merely an unforeseen byproduct that they seem to be a detriment to the development of unaided fields of instruction.

The widespread diffusion of governmental interest in research is another significant finding. A total of 28 different federal agencies sponsored at least one program in one or another of the 26 institutions of the Carnegie Study. Most of the research grants to these institutions came from six agencies: National Institutes of Health, Department of Defense, National Science Foundation, Atomic Energy Commission, Department of Agriculture, and National Aeronautics and Space Administration. Some of these same institutions are also involved as managers, alone or with others, of separately sponsored laboratories. Often, the laboratories require interinstitutional cooperation, such as Brookhaven managed by the Associated Universities.

To date, although numerous federal agencies have been dispensing funds of various sorts to institutions of higher learning, nowhere in the federal system is there any mechanism to monitor, coordinate, or create guiding policies in research. Similarly, no individual or agency is concerned with the whole problem of future involvements of the federal government in this realm.

The 500 participating colleges and universities, however, are equally uncoordinated, actually striving for funds in a very competitive field. Not only do the various recipients of federal funds maintain constant contacts in Washington, D.C., but the most successful of them expend considerable effort in maintaining friendly relations with officials who can influence the granting of research contracts.

Federal Programs for International Education

Although it is generally known that the federal government is interested in programs of international education, the extent of this involvement is difficult to ascertain. Certainly, it has more ramifications than are generally recognized. The Director of Foreign Policy Studies for the Brookings Institution has characterized the federal international education programs as "a heterogeneous and sometimes unruly flock of activities." The programs are scattered among 24 federal organizations, only eight of which are considered of major significance. Other investigators have found it extremely difficult to obtain a clear indication of the number of persons involved and of the amount of money expended.

There are reasons for this state of affairs. As in the case of all federal educational activities, the various programs are generated independently in many offices, and there is no unifying or coordinating agency. Moreover, although parts of the program are old, most of the activities were begun as recently as World War II. The same Brookings Institution authority states:

> One can scarcely recall the tranquil prewar era when the globe-trotting academic was a rarity and the government was quite unconcerned whether professors ventured abroad or stayed home tending their gardens and campus politics. During the seething postwar years, however, no red-blooded professor stays in his own country if he can possibly wangle his passage abroad, and the government has become a major entrepreneur in stimulating the growing worldwide traffic in students and teachers.[11]

President Kennedy said a month after his inauguration: "There is no better way of helping the new nations of Latin America, Africa, and Asia in their present pursuit of freedom and better living conditions than by assisting them to develop their human resources through education. Likewise there is no better way to strengthen our bonds of understanding and friendship with older nations than

---

[11] H. Field Haviland, Jr., "Federal Programs of International Education," in Charles G. Dobbins, *op. cit.*, p. 76.

through educational and cultural exchange." [12] Moreover, the President is endeavoring to bring order out of chaos by regarding the Secretary of State, aided by an Assistant Secretary and the Bureau of Educational and Cultural Affairs, as the agent for primary leadership "in persuading the members of the flock to move in more or less consistent directions." [13]

In addition to the Bureau of Educational and Cultural Affairs, the other seven major agencies involved in international education are the Agency for International Development, the Department of Defense, the United States Information Agency, the National Science Foundation, the Department of Health, Education, and Welfare, the National Aeronautics and Space Administration, and the Peace Corps. Others participate less extensively, such as the Department of the Interior and the Department of Labor.

The Cost of Direct Aid to Education

The various sorts of federal educational subventions for students for 1961 totaled $377,000,000. Of this amount, student financial assistance claimed $191,000,000; education and training programs, $73,000,000; research grants for the sole support of students, $64,000,000; and international activities involving student subventions, $49,000,000. The National Aeronautics and Space Administration, the Department of Agriculture, and other agencies maintained direct student aid programs not included in this figure.

It was estimated that the typical aided undergraduate received $690 that year and the typical graduate student, $3000. Nearly half the sum for undergraduates was in the form of loans, while almost all the money received by graduate students were grants not expected to be repaid.

Federal Programs for Capital Improvements

The first federal involvements in the area of capital improvements for colleges and universities were the Works Progress Administration and Public Works Administration programs during the depression years of the 1930's. The assistance to higher education was

---

[12] *Ibid.*
[13] *Ibid.*, p. 77.

incidental to the primary purpose of the program, which was to provide employment to the craftsmen, the victims of the depression. A total of $111,000,000 was expended on 664 college campuses.

After World War II, the Federal Public Housing Administration helped furnish buildings for the veterans who returned to the campus. Again, this was not strictly a manifestation of federal interest in education, but actually a form of reward to the veterans. Similarly, the Surplus Property Program that followed World War I and was continued and revived after World War II was not essentially an educational program, although since 1947 over $250,-000,000 worth of real and personal property have been transferred to the colleges and universities.

Most important to the colleges and universities have been the College Housing Loan Program and the large variety of research programs sponsored by the many governmental agencies. Since 1950, more than 70 per cent of the eligible colleges and universities in the nation have participated in the College Housing Loan Program, designed to assist them in housing students and faculty and to provide facilities related to such housing, including food service, infirmaries, and student unions. The loans extend for as long as 50 years at low interest rates, set by the prevailing rate at which the Treasury can borrow money for its own purposes. On July 1, 1962, it was 3½ per cent, but it had been as low as 2¾ per cent. A total of 1925 loans had been made by 1962, totaling over $2,000,-000,000. It is believed that housing has been furnished for 376,000 students, faculty, nurses, and interns. In addition, federal money has been expended for an additional 500 projects, including college unions, dining halls, and infirmaries. The 1961 Congress extended the program for four more years at an annual rate of $300,000,000.

Almost all departments of the federal government are authorized to finance research on college campuses, and frequently the various grants involve capital improvements. Most of the agencies involved have been mentioned previously: the National Science Foundation, the Department of Defense, the Department of Health, Education and Welfare, the Atomic Energy Commission, and the National Aeronautics and Space Administration. Additional agencies that can finance capital improvements include the Department of Agriculture, the Federal Aviation Agency, the Department of Commerce, National Bureau of Standards, the Office of Civil and Defense Mobilization, the Department of Interior, the Post Office Department, the Small Business Administration, the Department of State, the Veterans Administration, and possibly others. Apparently no calculation has been published of the total amount contributed by the federal government for capital improvements in colleges and universities. One prediction can be made with assurance: Such expenditures will continue.

Recently, the Urban Renewal Program, sponsored by the federal government, has provided funds to enable institutions of higher learning to acquire land through their local urban renewal organizations at costs lower than otherwise possible. Private schools that cannot exercise the power of eminent domain may purchase land through this program. Also, the Area Development Program, which is designed to assist depressed areas, has recently in a few instances furnished the funds for the construction of new buildings at colleges and universities in these areas.

The 87th Congress considered a major proposal to provide general assistance to colleges and universities for building programs; this failed of enactment in the closing days of the session in 1962. To date, no current program of the federal government has been directed at the most apparent needs in American colleges and universities: classrooms and libraries. Once again, the Federal Government has been dealing with a program of "bits and pieces," dictated by special interest groups. Meantime, it is estimated that American colleges and universities must invest at least $19,000,000,000 in capital improvements in the 1960's if adequate higher education is to be available in the 1970's. No solution to this problem is in sight that does not involve the federal government.

The problem of providing facilities for the American youth of the 1970's in the colleges and universities is complicated by the church-vs.-state controversy, and also by the private-vs.-public issue. The National Education Asociation, the Council of Chief State School Executives, and several other educational organizations and leaders are opposed to federal grants to church-related or private schools. On the other hand, the American Council on Education which includes private schools in its membership, as well as their numerous associations, favors federal funds for both public and private institutions. In the words of the Council: "The crucial issue is not how many dollars come from private sources and how many from public sources but whether or not the total of these dollars will be sufficient to meet the challenge colleges and universities face." In 1962 it still is not clear whether legislation to furnish capital improvements for public institutions alone can achieve Congressional approval, or whether private schools must be included in any successful legislative proposal.

Opposition to capital outlay from federal funds is related to the fear of federal control of higher education. This is a battle that has been going on in legislative halls for a century since the establishment of the land-grant colleges, but meantime Congress has furnished more and more money for higher education. Apparently, the fear is not well-founded, or the present programs are at fault and should be repealed, rather than expanded as they have been.

There is less fear of federal funds for capital improvements than of federal support for current educational programs. By the 1960's more than 40 per cent of the new dormitories and other revenue producing structures on college campuses were being constructed under the Housing Act of 1950. By 1963 the amount of these loans exceeded $2,000,000,000. Although not all colleges and universities have been willing to participate, more than a thousand have, with the result that 376,000 students are in federally financed structures a good many hours of each school day. Is it not conceivable that the college youth of the 1970's will be in classrooms and libraries, as well as research laboratories, financed in part by the federal government?

Some Questions of Future Policy

No longer does the United States Government ignore the needs of higher education. In fact, its contributions in recent years are breathtaking. It is no longer possible to theorize that the federal government has no business in higher education, that higher education is a state function and must be kept that way. In the 1960 fiscal year, it is estimated that the federal government spent about a billion dollars in the institutions of higher learning—$450,000,000 for research, $44,000,000 for facilities, $388,000,000 for scholarships and fellowships, and $217,000,000 for various programs of instruction. Moreover, these expenditures do not include the great sums for separate laboratories, the benefits to the institutions of sharing government surplus property, or the increasing student loans. The addition of the money involved in these last ventures would almost double the total expenditure.

No longer is the participation of the federal government an academic question. The most important current scientific research studies are carried on under government auspices. The great outlay for scientific research and research facilities is a significant contribution of the federal government to the times; the research objectives would be unattainable by any other means. In fact, the federal government has become a major source of operating revenue in higher education, especially for some institutions with elaborate graduate programs.

Unquestionably, the participation of the federal government in higher education has been a good thing. It has stimulated research; it has built and helped build the great laboratories of the space age, both off campus and on campus; it has provided programs and loans to help students to attend school and remain there longer; and it has stimulated faculty and student exchanges with foreign countries.

At the same time, there is another side to the story. The main outcry from the American colleges has been in criticism of the red tape that has been forced upon them. The research professor becomes a business executive and politician, preparing and taking action on applications, making elaborate reports on the uses to which the funds have been put, and administering the projects in progress.

Many university officials have had a sad awakening when they have first realized that the government grants do not cover the full cost of the research the government sponsors, that training personnel for the Peace Corps forces the sponsoring institution to meet payrolls out of local resources long before government money is forthcoming, that certain departments and professors who least need the additional moneys are the first to get it, that some of the university departments have a great deal of money while other departments do not have enough, that science flourishes while the humanities suffer, that laboratories expand while libraries remain static, that the foreign students bring problems that administrators must somehow find faculty time to meet.

As a whole, the faculty members are more concerned about departmental imbalances that follow federal grants. Some are worried about whether faculty members are going to have much to say about their own research projects. Some professors are more loyal to the federal government than they are to the local college departments and institutions. Some administrators worry about the proper instruction of the undergraduates as one professor after another obtains a research grant. As President Pusey of Harvard has said:

> Basically and most important, will the new and growing association with government strengthen or weaken our educational institutions in their ability to perform their essential work? The answer to this question will be found only in a multiplicity of responses given over a long period of time to a host of related, more pointed queries. Will future Government regulatory policies adequately recognize the true nature of educational institutions? Or will they simply treat colleges and universities as service agencies in particular situations?

> Will Government recognize that education is as properly a matter for national concern as are defense, health, and technical and economic advance? Will the Government's programs make proper allowance for basic as well as for applied research? And for teaching? Will Government recognize how important it is that an institution of higher learning strive to advance simultaneously and consistently along a broad front of academic interests rather than be content to make occasional spurts ahead in some limited area of immediate concern? Will leaders of Government actively support, not merely pay lip service to, the idea that the social studies and the humanities are also relevant in considerations of national strength?

> A further serious matter: Will programs of the Government affecting higher education show proper care not to weaken the bastions against political interference which educational leaders have been slowly building through centuries? Will they recognize that to realize its purpose a college or university must have the final say over the nature and direction of its educational and investigative activities?

> Will government programs be adequately sensitive to the fact that good education and good research require steadfast concern for standards of excellence, and that neither will be achieved if it becomes a guiding aim of Government programs to keep everyone happy and to avoid hard choices? From the other side, will colleges and universities recognize that they have to change to meet new needs? Will they organize themselves to work cooperatively with agencies of Government, ceasing to go their own ways and to contend selfishly among themselves? Will they also concede that they have an obligation to work with Government, not only to advance knowledge but also to extend educational opportunity? More par-

ticularly, will representatives of the institutions of higher education find effective ways to sit down with informed and concerned representatives from Government to evolve wise policies, and then—even more important—to get them understood in the Congress and in the country at large?

A new, complicated, imperfect but incalculably significant—and promising—relationship between the Federal Government and institutions of higher learning has grown up during the past two decades almost without direction. The overreaching question it now raises for us all is how to work together in the years immediately ahead to perfect this relationship in both education's and the nation's interest. Can we, for example, in this next period find some more considerable middle ground between the present largely mission-oriented Federal programs on the one hand and an unwanted and dangerous program of general Federal support for higher education on the other? This is the big question which must be answered in a multitude of smaller decisions.[14]

At the same conference at which President Pusey raised these questions, McGeorge Bundy, a White House aide and former Harvard dean, anticipated the questions and gave the official government response. His contention was that without the federal money, the university scientists could not have done the things they have done in the last fifteen years. He said, "It is no good to talk about academic freedom when antiquated laboratories, inadequate instruments, and overcrowded teaching schedules make serious inquiry impossible. When it is not given under crippling limitations and restrictions, money is quite simply an instrument of freedom, in the universities as well as elsewhere in life." [15]

Obviously, the question of States' Rights comes into the picture. Recently the Governor of Mississippi tried to interpose the authority of the state between its university and the federal government in an area in which the Supreme Court holds the federal government has supremacy. He soon learned, in the words of Chief Justice Charles Evan Hughes, "There is no . . . avenue of escape from the paramount authority of the Federal Constitution." There can be no question that the states have in recent decades voluntarily accepted an increasing dependence on the federal government in obtaining

---

[14] Nathan M. Pusey, "The Carnegie Study of the Federal Government and Higher Education," in Charles G. Dobbins, *op. cit.,* pp. 27–29.

[15] McGeorge Bundy, "Of Winds and Windmills: Free Universities and Public Policy," in Charles G. Dobbins, *op. cit.,* p. 91.

funds to carry on various programs, and there is probably no better example of this tendency than the new relationships that have evolved in the last few decades between state colleges and universities and the federal government.

CHAPTER VI

Crucial Problems in
State Higher Education

State-supported colleges and universities in every state have made much progress toward educational excellence. The pre-eminence of several of the state universities has been the spectacular achievement of only slightly more than a century of evolution; but the recent expansion and improvement of curriculums in the land-grant colleges and normal schools is a development of equal importance, compressed into a much briefer period. In the process of these evolutions, many practical and theoretical solutions have been achieved at the same time that new problems of function, relationship, and control were being recognized.

The Control of State Colleges and Universities

State institutions of higher education are controlled by a variety of political entities; the different eras of their establishment and the different regions of the nation have influenced the patterns of board organization and the scope of board powers over the administration, financing, curriculum, and personnel policies of the institutions. As one studies patterns of control in state colleges and universities, he can not avoid the conclusion that there is an intimate and necessary relationship between the degree of autonomy granted to a university and the quality of its faculty, the excellence of its curriculum, the scope of its educational services to the commonwealth and to the world, and its world-wide reputation for research, scholarship, and professional preparation. If this is a valid conclusion, the implications for future legislation in all of the states are inescapable: The trend must be toward investing state universities and colleges with autonomy commensurate with their responsibilities.

As this trend toward autonomy progresses, decisions will be

reached in several areas of governmental and educational operation. One of the basic decisions must deal with the relationship of higher education to the political agencies of the state. In some of the states, colleges are still controlled by one of the departments of the state government, with political leadership at the top and civil servants as administrators of such matters as architectural development, budget preparation, purchasing, personnel policies, promotions, and other functions that affect the quality of education vitally, even though indirectly. In other states, a lay board of trustees or regents may bear the responsibility for institutional policies, but may find that its authority is circumscribed by allowing routine decisions on expenditures to be made by minor officials in a state treasurer's or state auditor's office over whom the board has no influence and no control.

At the other end of the scale of independence from political influence are the universities in six states that "have given constitutional autonomy to the institution for the purpose of protecting it from caprices of public or political interference and from having to accept staff appointments on the basis of political patronage. In yet other states, autonomy has been given to the university by legislative act." [1] The Committee on Government and Higher Education approves the view that "once the state machinery is employed to determine what share of the state's financial resources shall be allocated to higher education, and the appropriation has been made, the management of expenditures shall be the responsibility of the university. Through its governing board, the university shall in turn be held accountable for the wise and frugal use of these public funds in meeting the academic goals of the institution." [2]

The composition and power of the boards of regents present another aspect of control of higher education that has bearing on quality. Here also several patterns have been established in the fifty states, and some of the patterns seem to encourage better education than others. A longer term of office for members of the lay board seems more effective than a shorter one, not only because it enables the trustee to achieve a familiarity with problems and personnel and a feeling of identification with the institution, but also because

---

[1] The Committee on Government and Higher Education, *The Efficiency of Freedom* (Baltimore, Md.: The Johns Hopkins Press, 1959), pp. 4–5.
[2] *Ibid.*, p. 15.

the longer term effectively prohibits any governor from gaining control over the entire board. In several recent state surveys of higher education, appointed boards are recommended to replace elected boards, on the grounds that many able citizens who would serve by appointment would be unwilling to compete for election in an expensive political contest. In addition, by appointment it is possible to make certain that important points of view are represented on the board.[3]

A more vexing decision about boards of regents for higher education concerns the number of such boards within a state and the number of institutions each can control. In a state with small population and only two or three institutions of higher education, the decision to have a single board for all state-supported colleges or separate boards for each may seem purely a matter of choice or convenience. In the larger states with varieties of institutions, some of which have multiple campuses, the nature of the lay board is of greater consequence. A single board of regents for all of higher education in a state can be supported on the basis that it will permit harmonious and coordinated development of all of the needed aspects of higher education. On the other hand, in a state with a half million students in 50 or more universities and colleges of several types, a single board can be overwhelmed by the number of decisions it must make with inadequate information. Each institution may feel itself to be too remote from the sources of power, and it is possible that the university may be favored unduly at the expense of other units in the system.

The opposite extreme, a separate board for each separate campus, has advantages in that many citizens can share in the establishment of policy for higher education, and each institution can feel that its problems receive the undivided attention of a responsible board. In the larger states, however, this plan would lead to uneven development of institutions, to unseemly competition among institutions, and perhaps to excessive duplication of programs and to excessive costs of operation. Some grouping of institutions under separate lay boards seems necessary, but questions of the best number of institutions per board, the ranking of boards by degree of auton-

---

[3] John Dale Russell, *Higher Education in Michigan: The Final Report of the Survey of Higher Education in Michigan* (Lansing, Mich.: The Michigan Legislative Study Committee on Higher Education, 1958), p. 105.

omy and authority, and the coordination of their efforts in the interest of educational quality and of economy still remain unresolved. After considering all state boards in the nation, Martorana and Hollis conclude: "If a fresh start could be taken in a State having nine or more public colleges, the authors would argue for a system to place each institutional unit, whether a 2-year college or a 4-year institution or a complex university, under its own governing board, and over this board, a statewide coordinating board with major duties of interinstitutional programming, budget coordination, and long-range planning." [4] Their recommendation has not yet been adopted universally.

A third problem of control (the first was the proper legal status of institutions of higher education, and the second was the proper relation of boards to multiple institutions) is the nature of the presidency of universities and colleges. Should the president be professor or businessman? How can he possibly be both? The wry comment, "An eminent scientist has been ruined to make a mediocre president," can be balanced by equally disillusioned evaluations of the effectiveness of the lawyer or industrialist as college president. The president must serve as the point of contact between the faculty, the board of regents, and the public. He needs to be able to earn the respect, to speak the language, and to merit the support of all three groups. Some efforts have been made to establish training schools for administrators of colleges. The task is complex and there is as yet no evidence to indicate that these training programs have been able to produce administrators with conspicuously successful records.

After he has been chosen, from whatever background that may recommend him to the regents and to the faculty, the president still finds it difficult to arrive at a clear description of his powers. Is he autocrat or servant? If servant, are his services devoted primarily to the regents and the public or to the faculty and the students? Must he be beggar at the legislature and before foundations and boards, or must he be educational statesman, gathering an outstanding faculty and inspiring them to continued research, publication, and teaching? Is it possible that the different sorts of state institutions of higher education require different qualities of presidents, and that

---

[4] S. V. Martorana and Ernest V. Hollis, *State Boards Responsible for Higher Education* (Washington, D.C.: Government Printing Office, 1960), p. 49.

job descriptions would vary for the university president and the state college president? The personality and competence of the institutional chief are crucial to educational effectiveness; more thought needs to be given to his choice and his function after selection.

Finally, the place of the faculty in the control of higher education is in a state of flux, complicated by the prospective shortage of fully qualified faculty members. Ideally, the university is a community of scholars; each member of the faculty is a professional person, fully educated, and competent in his field. No one is more competent than the faculty to settle questions of curriculum and instruction. The functions of management and administration are separated from instruction solely for convenience, and not because they require rarer competence or more intensive preparation. The president and the deans are simply spokesmen for their peers, first among equals. The concept of labor and management, of employer and employee, simply does not accord with the facts, if the university or the college is properly managed and properly staffed.

In many American colleges, especially in those that were not the original university of their state, this ideal relationship has never yet been achieved. Too many of them were established and continued as petty dictatorships. They are only now evolving the procedures and policies that will assign to the faculties the responsibilities for policy that they can discharge effectively and efficiently, while they cooperate with boards of regents and presidents in allocating each function to the agency that can best perform it. Of all of the problems of control to be solved over the coming decades, the role of the faculty in the administration of higher education seems likely to be the most difficult.

Coordination Among Institutions

Increasing numbers of students and institutions, increasing similarity of institutional objectives both in specialized programs and in liberal arts, the rising costs of higher education, the shortage of qualified instructors, and the importance of adequate opportunity for higher education—all indicate the necessity for careful planning and coordination of effort within each state and region. The importance of the problem is underscored by the report that since

1957 provision for some type of survey of the facilities, finances, programs, or administration of higher education has been enacted by the legislatures of 31 states. Twenty-one states undertook such studies during 1961 alone.[5] Details of the need for coordination are presented in Chapter II.

Adequate Support

For all of higher education, the United States spends annually about $4 billion; the American Assembly reports estimates of needed annual expenditures by 1970 ranging from a low of $9½ billion to a high of $13 billion for current operation, plus funds for capital expansion totaling from a low estimate of $15 billion for the decade to a high estimate of $33 billion.[6] State-supported colleges and universities will require the greatest proportion of these increases, because they must absorb the greatest proportion of the increases in student enrollment.

The same report of the American Assembly presents an estimate of the sources of income for educational institutions in 1957–58. The estimate for 669 public institutions indicated that their revenues were derived in the main from governmental sources (77.5 per cent), tuition and fees (7.9 per cent), gifts and grants (2.9 per cent), and other sources such as contracted services (10.8 per cent). For these public institutions, endowments accounted for only 0.9 per cent of income.[7] From which sources are the needed increases likely to come over the next decade?

A trend that causes concern to some students of higher education is toward marked increases in fees in public colleges and universities. The main justification for such increases is the argument that since the student benefits most from higher education, he should be expected to pay more of the cost. It seems inevitable that fees and tuition for public higher education will continue to rise as they have done in the past several years, if only to maintain the present share of expenditures that is borne by the student. At the same time, it

[5] S. V. Martorana and Ernest V. Hollis, *Survey of State Legislation Relating to Higher Education, January 1, 1961 to December 31, 1961,* Office of Education Circular No. 684 (Washington, D.C.: Government Printing Office, 1962), p. 10.
[6] The American Assembly, *The Federal Government and Higher Education* (Englewood Cliffs, N.J.: Prentice-Hall, Inc., 1960), p. 144.
[7] *Ibid.*

seems unlikely that these charges can be increased sufficiently to provide for most of the needed increase in expenditures. Tuition and fees currently account for eight per cent of the income of public colleges; to attain important gains in total income from students would require these items to be increased five or even ten times. Such an increase, even over a decade, is unlikely.

In the first place, major increases in these charges would exclude even more gifted students from college; they would force others to work a greater part of the time to earn their way, and so would delay their graduation and dilute their education. The social and economic importance of a high level of education argues against increasing the financial barriers to education unless there is no other possible way to provide for it. In addition, tuition and fees are only a part of the cost of attending college. The costs of board and room, books, travel, and incidentals amount to several times present tuition costs. The student and his family ordinarily bear these inescapable costs, as well as the loss of earnings while he is in college. All these considerations indicate that income from students is unlikely to bear a significantly greater share of the expenses of public higher education than it now does.

For public institutions, gifts, grants, and endowments are unlikely sources of markedly increased income. All together they amounted in 1957–58 to less than four per cent of current income in public colleges, although they are very important factors in the income of private colleges, and increases in their total amounts should ordinarily be channeled to these institutions, rather than to public ones. Certainly it would seem that philanthropy is an uncertain and inappropriate foundation for the long-range support and expansion of state-supported higher education.

Taxation then remains the only feasible major source for increases in income, just as it accounts at present for almost four-fifths of current income for public higher education. To recognize this fact, however, is not necessarily to make it a reality. Questions of public policy are involved in increasing the tax support of colleges and universities. What tax sources can be found to provide this support? How can states with lower per capita income be encouraged to provide adequate college education? How much should the wealthier states contribute to the support of nation-wide higher education? In view of the extent of educational need and the mobility of the population, can the nation afford to continue its diversified, competitive, and in some ways inefficient state-controlled system of higher education? Or will it seem inevitable that a federally organized and supported plan for higher education take over in order to equalize both opportunity for higher education and the burden of its costs? Assuming the continuance of present control, what patterns of federal support of higher education are desirable, workable, and necessary?

These are but a few of the problems of support of higher education that must be solved as enrollments increase. Coordinated support and coordinated planning seem to be prerequisite to efficient and economical support of the great expansion of higher education that is inevitable. Some exploration of alternatives has been undertaken, but definitive and comprehensive proposals have not yet been elaborated.

Faculty Supply

The supply of qualified faculty is related to the problem of financial support, even though factors other than financial are more important. The shortage of instructors affects all higher education, private as well as public. Thus in all higher education in America, the annual need for new full-time instructors to care for growth and replacement is estimated at 28,000 at present, rising to 36,000 by 1970.[8] The annual number of earned doctorates awarded has been about a third of the current need for new teachers, and by no means all of the new holders of doctoral degrees become new college teachers. Some go into industry and government, and others are already teaching. Every year, almost three-fourths of new college teachers have less than the desired doctoral preparation; the likelihood is that their level of preparation will decline annually for several years. The prospective deficit therefore is not only in numbers, but also in the quality of the faculty in higher education.

Several suggestions have been advanced for an alleviation of the shortage. Accelerated programs of preparation involving a specialized two-year graduate degree for college teachers have been insti-

---

[8] *Teacher Supply and Demand in Universities, Colleges, and Junior Colleges, 1959–60 and 1960–61,* Research Report 1961 R–12 (Washington, D.C.: National Education Association, 1961), p. 53.

tuted in several universities. Campaigns to improve the recruitment of women, retired professors, or part-time instructors from industry have met with limited success. Increases in average salaries have had some influence on the attractiveness of college teaching as a career, even though professorial salaries are still competitively low. Efforts by professors to identify able undergraduates and to encourage them to consider careers in college teaching would be helpful, even though their full effect would be delayed for several years until graduate study could be completed. Unless this problem can be solved, effective coordination and control of higher education and more generous financial support will fail of their primary purposes.

Improved Instruction

The two problems of faculty recruitment and of improving the quality of instruction exist together in both private and public institutions, and the problems are not unrelated. It may be that more effective techniques of instruction, placing more responsibility for learning on the student, could be a major contribution to alleviating the expected shortages. American colleges generally believe in a great deal of personal contact between professor and student, and they judge their effectiveness in part by the ratio of professors to students. The seminar, the tutorial, the small discussion group, and the opportunity for the student to confer with his professors are parts of the American ideal of a college education, even though the lecture is most widely used.

This pattern places the responsibility for the learning activity largely on the professor, whereas the student is relegated to the position of recipient. Many European observers charge this system with pampering and paternalism. They feel that it inhibits the growth of independent scholarship in American students. Whether or not the American system is better suited to the education of a high proportion of young people than the European practice is, it seems probable that the pressure of numbers of students may cause major changes in student-faculty ratios and in methods of instruction, more acutely in public than in private colleges. The challenge to ingenuity will be to develop changes that may possibly improve the quality of educational opportunity even in the face of faculty shortages.

The development of electronic communications has led to the

hope that the influence of the exceptionally talented professor can be extended to unlimited numbers of students, even in distant colleges or in later semesters, at the same time that the student is required to be more aggressive in searching out sources and in solving his own learning problems. The film, the radio, and the public-address system were first steps in this extension of the professor's audience. The influences of closed-circuit or microwave television and of the video tape can be only conjectured as yet. The only certainty is that their use will have dangers, as well as opportunities, for the quality of education, and that it can lead to repetition and rote learning as easily as to creativity and inspiration. New techniques can, if wisely used, be a means to the improvement of instruction for the growing numbers of students. Legislators and administrators who see in mass communications only a way to economize will miss the point. The use of new media must be planned to be both effective and economical.

Other techniques are being discussed as means to improve instruction. Independent study, honors courses, advanced standing for more able entering students, and opportunities to receive credit by examination have been proposed as methods by which the motivation and involvement of students might be increased. Each of these methods has proved to be effective with limited numbers of students; each is likely to be more expensive than conventional methods; and each demands more time and ingenuity of the professor than the lecture or the laboratory. It is conceivable that some combination of information and interpretation through television, coupled with interaction and stimulation through small-group personal contact, may prove to be the pathway to excellent instruction for great numbers of students. It is the problem of the state-supported universities and colleges to find the appropriate combination to achieve both objectives.

Student Selection

The dilemma of selectivity in state-supported higher education is to make certain that opportunity is made available to every qualified student, and at the same time to define the term "qualified" for each state-supported institution in such a way as to eliminate those applicants who can not benefit from the programs offered by it. Several of the states admit to state universities and colleges any graduate of an accredited high school in the state, and they protect standards by a high rate of disqualification after the first term. In other states, a hierarchy of admission standards is established to permit a very high degree of self-selection for higher education and, at the same time, to provide increasingly rigorous competition in the several kinds of higher educational institutions. The latter policy seems to be a more realistic adaptation to the ideal of equality of educational opportunity, since it both expands the range of opportunity and encourages attendance at college for as long as the student is successful and finds the course worthwhile.

Relations to the People of the State

The state-supported college or university ordinarily began with a clear understanding of its dependence upon the supporting commonwealth and of its functions in relation to the people of the state. The paths to eminence among universities, however, lead away from a close relationship to local communities. One of the fundamental problems now facing state institutions is that of defining their roles in relation to their original local functions of service on the one hand, and the emerging universality and independence on the other. The striving for excellence as defined by the faculty seems inevitably to widen the gulf between the college and its constituency, and so to endanger the popular support that makes possible the growth and expansion of the institution.

Higher education is coming to be an inflexible requirement for employment and a highly desirable preparation for effective American citizenship for as many as half of all young people. The states and their people have established their colleges and universities, as they see the matter, precisely in order that higher education may be provided for those who need it. The increase in this need from four per cent of all youth to 50 per cent is, it seems to them, a detail that does not change the essential nature of the assigned task. Faculty members see the matter differently. They would prefer to teach the able, the eager, and the well prepared; and some of them would prefer to teach only those who are competent as research assistants and who plan to specialize in the professor's discipline. Greater numbers of students seem to many of them to be a distraction from the proper concentration on research, publication, and professional preparation of graduate students. What they feel it important to teach, they insist, simply cannot be taught to most of the young people who apply for admission. These attitudes toward enrollments form one facet of the problem of the relation of the university to its community.

Research is another function of the university that is seen differently by the faculty and the community. The community tends to expect results to be immediate, practical, understandable, and of financial value. For such research, there is never difficulty in securing appropriations. Research to improve the yield of corn, the efficiency of fuel, or the health of children is clearly in the tradition of the land-grant colleges. The university tradition has been to seek for understanding without respect for immediate utility. The university tradition recognizes that much research will be fruitless, or fruitful only in the negative sense of proving that an hypothesis was erroneous. As state universities recruit distinguished faculties and construct more specialized laboratories and libraries, more and more of their research will be of this fundamental remote sort, seemingly unrelated to the daily problems of the citizen. The problem of relationships is that of maintaining the understanding and support of the citizen for activities that are central to the concept of the university, no matter how little they may mean to him.

This clear-cut divergence of interest has been blurred of late years by the growth of contract research. When government or industry offers a contract to a university for research leading toward the eventual solution of a practical problem in public health, national defense, or business policy, the contract has widespread effects on the relations between the university and its constituency. The financial dependence on state funds is lessened, at least a little. The note of practicality is introduced into the laboratory. The independent direction of their scholarly activities is removed to some extent from the faculty and the trustees to the agency that poses the problem and provides the money. The interest of faculty members in their own pure research is interfered with, and the proportion of time and effort devoted to undergraduate instruction is similarly diluted. Buildings, business managers, research assistants, and custodians are added to the university, thus becoming a charge on its general funds after the contract has expired. The problem once more is one of balance. Such contract research is an added function for colleges and universities that cannot avoid interfering with their previous functions. How can the untoward effects of that interference be minimized, and the advantages to the university, its faculty, its students, and its commonwealth be maximized?

The entire system of state colleges and universities in the United States forms a monument to the vitality of the democratic ideal in a pluralistic society. The problems of the system press for solution, even though they will be replaced by others. In spite of—or possibly because of—important imperfections in their theory, planning, support, and practices, these institutions have made essential contributions to American life. The next decades will see them consolidate and improve their standards of intellectual excellence and of comprehensive educational service.

Bibliography

Allen, Hollis K. and Richard G. Axt, *State Public Finance and State Institutions of Higher Education in the United States.* New York: Columbia University Press, 1952.

Association of Land-Grant Colleges and Universities, *The Land-Grant Institutions and Their Relationships to Federal, State and Local Government: A Report to the Commission on Intergovernmental Relations.* Washington, D.C.: The Association, 1954.

Babbidge, Homer D., *The Federal Interest in Higher Education.* New York: McGraw-Hill Book Company, Inc., 1962.

Brody, Alexander, *The American State and Higher Education (The Legal, Political, and Constitutional Relationships).* Washington, D.C.: American Council on Education, 1935.

Brubacher, John S. and Willis Rudy, *Higher Education in Transition: An American History, 1639–1956.* New York: Harper & Row, Publishers, 1957.

Butts, R. Freeman, *The College Charts Its Course.* New York: McGraw-Hill Book Company, Inc., 1939.

Carstensen, Vernon, "A Century of the Land-Grant Colleges," *Journal of Higher Education,* No. 33 (January, 1962), 30–37.

Committee on Government and Higher Education, *The Efficiency of Freedom.* Baltimore, Md.: Johns Hopkins Press, 1959.

Council of State Governments, *Higher Education in the Forty-Eight States* (A Report to the Governor's Conference, 1952). Chicago: The Council of State Governments, 1952.

Diekhoff, John S., *Democracy's College: Higher Education in the Local Community.* New York: Harper & Row, Publishers, 1950.

Dobbins, Charles G., ed., *Higher Education and the Federal Government: Programs and Problems.* Washington, D.C.: American Council on Education, 1963.

Dodds, Harold Willis, *The Academic President: Educator or Caretaker?* New York: McGraw-Hill Book Company, Inc., 1962.

Eddy, Edward D., Jr., *Colleges for Our Land and Time: The Land-Grant Idea in American Education.* New York: Harper & Row, Publishers, 1957.

Foerster, Norman, *The American State University.* Chapel Hill, N.C.: University of North Carolina Press, 1937.

Frederick, William L., *The States and Higher Education.* Chicago: The Council of State Governments, 1957.

101

Glenny, Lyman, *Autonomy of Public Colleges*. New York: McGraw-Hill Book Company, Inc., 1959.

Havighurst, Robert J., *American Higher Education in the 1960's*. Columbus, Ohio: Ohio State University Press, 1960.

Henderson, Algo D., *Policies and Practices in Higher Education*. New York: Harper & Row, Publishers, 1960

Hofstadter, Richard and C. DeWitt Hardy, *The Development and Scope of Higher Education in the United States*. New York: Columbia University Press, 1952.

Hofstadter, Richard and Wilson Smith, *American Higher Education: A Documentary History* (2 vols.). Chicago: University of Chicago Press, 1961.

Holmes, Dwight Oliver Wendell, *The Evolution of the Negro College*, Contributions to Education No. 609. New York: Bureau of Publications, Teachers College, Columbia University, 1934.

Irwin, Mary K., ed., *American Universities and Colleges, 1960*, 8th ed. Washington, D.C.: American Council on Education, 1960.

Kidd, Charles V., *American Universities and Federal Research*. Cambridge, Mass.: Harvard University Press, 1959.

Klein, Arthur J., *Survey of Land-Grant Colleges and Universities* (2 vols.), U.S. Office of Education Bulletin 1930, No. 9. Washington, D.C.: Government Printing Office, 1930.

A Master Plan for Higher Education in California, 1960–1975. Sacramento, Calif.: California State Department of Education, 1960.

Martorana, S. V. and Ernest V. Hollis, *State Boards Responsible for Higher Education,* U.S. Office of Education Circular No. 619. Washington, D.C.: Government Printing Office, 1960.

————, *Survey of State Legislation Relating to Higher Education,* U.S. Office of Education Circulars. Washington, D.C.: Government Printing Office, annually.

McNeely, John H., *Higher Educational Institutions in the Scheme of State Government,* U.S. Office of Education Bulletin 1939, No. 3. Washington, D.C.: Government Printing Office, 1939.

Moos, Malcolm and F. E. Rourke, *The Campus and the State*. Baltimore, Md.: Johns Hopkins University Press, 1958.

Nevins, Allan, *The State Universities and Democracy*. Urbana, Ill.: University of Illinois Press, 1962.

1962–1963 College Facts Chart. Spartanburg, S.C.: The National Beta Club, 1962.

Opening (Fall) Enrollment in Higher Education, 1962: Institutional Data, U.S. Office of Education Circular No. 697. Washington, D.C.: Government Printing Office, annual editions.

Orlans, Harold, *The Effects of Federal Programs on Higher Education*. Washington, D.C.: The Brookings Institution, 1962.

The Report of the Governor's Commission on Education Beyond the High School. Raleigh, N.C.: The Governor's Commission, 1962.

Ross, Earle D., "The Great Triumvirate of Land-Grant Educators," *Journal of Higher Education*, No. 32 (December, 1961), 480–88.

———, *Democracy's College: The Land-Grant Movement in the Formative Stage*. Ames, Iowa: Iowa State College Press, 1942.

Russell, John Dale, *The Financing of Higher Education*. Chicago: University of Chicago Press, 1954.

Sanford, R. Nevitt, ed., *The American College*. New York: John Wiley & Sons, Inc., 1962.

Thackrey, Russell I. and Jay Richter, "The Land-Grant Colleges and Universities, 1862–1962: An American Institution," *Higher Education*, Vol. 16, No. 3 (November, 1959), 3–8.

Thompson, Ronald B., *Enrollment Projections for Higher Education, 1961–1978*. Washington, D.C.: American Council on Education, 1961.

Wilkins, Theresa Birch, ed., *Education Directory 1962–1963, Part 3: Higher Education*. Washington, D.C.: Government Printing Office, 1963.

Appendix A

The classified lists in Appendix A were developed first by reference to the *1961–1962 College Facts Chart,* published annually by the National Beta Club, Spartanburg, South Carolina. Enrollments are those reported in *Opening (Fall) Enrollment in Higher Education, 1961: Institutional Data,* the annual publication of the Office of Education. The list of state universities and colleges was next checked with the analysis in "Table 1. — State Boards Responsible for Public Higher Education and Names of Institutional Units for Which They are Responsible, By Type," in S. V. Martorana and Ernest V. Hollis, *State Boards Responsible for Higher Education,* Washington: Government Printing Office, 1960.

Since none of these basic references proved to be infallible in classification, and sometimes disagreed on whether to list an institutional unit separately or under the parent university, frequent reference was made to Mary Irwin's *American Universities and Colleges* (eighth edition), and to Edmund J. Gleazer's *American Junior Colleges* (fifth edition), both published by the American Council on Education, 1960. In spite of these precautions, it seems likely that some disagreement with other listings and some errors of classification of institutional units, dates of founding, or Fall 1961 enrollments will be found in this list. Conscientious effort has been exerted to keep such errors at a minimum. The authors feel that the data are sufficiently accurate to justify confidence in the totals and any generalizations based on the classified list.

Definitions: State universities and colleges are considered to be those that are both controlled and supported by agencies of the state. This definition does not always permit a clear-cut decision on a given institution, but the doubtful instances are very few. More difficult classifications involved the offshoots of long-established institutional units, some of which have grown very rapidly in importance and in size in their states. An attempt was made to resolve this problem by listing as a single institution campuses that bore the same generic name, had the same governing board, and were established first as branches or offshoots of a parent institution.

In harmony with this principle, the specialized colleges of the State University of New York and the Pennsylvania two-year extension centers are listed as single institutions, although the state teachers colleges in both states are separately listed because of their separate establishments. In California, where the authors are closely acquainted with the institutions of higher education, the classification was especially difficult because of recent changes in control of the state colleges under the "Master Plan for Higher Education." Although these former teachers colleges are now under a common board of trustees, their establishments were separate, and they are listed separately in this classification. The University of California, on the other hand, has been considered an integral institution; many of its operations are centralized in the University offices, not on the several campuses. In accordance with the decision reached for New York, Pennsylvania, and other similar state situations, the University of California is listed as a single unit.

The classifications also may be subject to interpretation, in part because of trends reported in the text that are eliminating distinctions between institutions that were very clear at their first establishment. In accordance with other practice, six major categories of institutions are recognized:

State Universities are those state-supported institutions that first bore the name of university. Often they are also the first college established within a state, especially in states formed after the original thirteen states.

Land-Grant State Universities are listed separately from state universities. These are state universities to which the grants and the responsibilities established by the Morrill Act were assigned. They are reported separately here as in other discussions so that the statistics may be joined either with state universities or with land-grant colleges, as appropriate.

Separate Land-Grant Institutions. Forty-two institutions other than state universities were assigned Morrill Act grants and responsibilities; nearly all were established after 1862. Half of them now bear the title of university, and others have begun to discharge university functions. In several of the states, these foundations of the last 100 years now rival or surpass in quality and in prestige the originally established university of the state.

Normal Schools to Universities. This classification is the most numerous of the institutional types, because of the practice of many states in the last half of the 19th century of establishing regional normal schools. With recent growth in demand for higher education, these institutions have expanded and lengthened their curriculums so that they now combine liberal arts purposes and graduate study with their original task of preparing teachers. Their names progressed from "normal school" to "state teachers college" to "state college" and in thirteen of the 195 institutions to "state university."

State Junior Colleges. Most public junior colleges are controlled by locally elected governing boards. In several states, the university has established two-year extension or resident centers, controlled and staffed from the central home of the university. These are classified as part of the university. In addition, there are 36 state established, supported, and controlled junior colleges. Because of the specialized purpose of some of these colleges, it is likely that they will become four-year colleges when enrollment makes it possible. Others might conceivably be transferred to local control after the manner of most community colleges. It seems probable that the number of 36 will decrease in the future rather than increase, unless some such pattern as area vocational colleges becomes popular.

Other Colleges and Universities. Sixty-one state-supported and controlled colleges and universities did not fit any of the other categories.

There are eight institutions that were begun as two-year colleges between the years 1922 and 1948, but now have become baccalaureate-degree colleges and even universities. Seventeen single-purpose institutions still retain their specialized titles, even though several have become multipurpose institutions. Thirteen of this group were established during the nineteenth century, the oldest being the Medical College of South Carolina (1823); the youngest is the Maine Maritime Academy (1941).

Only five state-supported colleges for women remain, all founded in the South between 1884 and 1908. Two multipurpose colleges, in addition, were established as women's colleges but have recently become coeducational. Another group of 22 agricultural and technological colleges were established mostly between 1873 and 1923, with one addition in 1949.

A final group includes both the oldest and the youngest (in 1962) public institutions, the College of William and Mary (1693) and the University of South Florida (1956). Interesting examples of this miscellaneous category are Pembroke State College that began as a normal school for Indians in 1887, but now is a multipurpose institution; and Texas Western College, originally established as Texas School of Mines. The entire sub-group of sixty-one institutions gives further evidence of the diversity and flexibility of state-supported institutions of higher education.

	Founding Date	Fall 1961 Enrollment
Institution		
STATE UNIVERSITIES		
University of Alabama	1820	14,164
University of Colorado	1861	18,603
University of Georgia	1785	10,440
Indiana University	1820	28,975
State University of Iowa	1847	11,701
University of Kansas	1865	10,791
University of Michigan	1817	28,775
University of Mississippi	1844	5,339
Montana State University	1893	4,165
University of New Mexico	1889	8,213
University of North Carolina	1789	10,021
University of North Dakota	1883	4,582
Miami University (Ohio)	1809	10,858
Ohio University	1804	12,258
University of Oklahoma	1890	12,525
University of Oregon	1876	9,865
University of South Carolina	1801	7,452
State University of South Dakota	1882	2,712
University of Texas	1881	23,368
University of Utah	1850	12,071
University of Virginia	1819	10,321
University of Washington	1861	23,244
	Total	280,443
LAND-GRANT STATE UNIVERSITIES		
University of Alaska	1922	2,990
University of Arizona	1885	13,894
University of Arkansas	1871	7,373
University of California (all campuses)	1868	54,975
University of Connecticut	1881	12,132
University of Delaware	1833	6,377
University of Florida	1853	15,329
University of Hawaii	1907	10,250
University of Idaho	1889	4,530
University of Illinois	1867	32,088
University of Kentucky	1865	10,597
Louisiana State University and A and M College	1860	16,070
University of Maine	1865	6,183
University of Maryland	1807	24,386
University of Massachusetts	1863	6,624
University of Minnesota	1851	42,130
University of Missouri	1839	16,205
University of Nebraska	1869	9,436
University of Nevada	1874	4,738
University of New Hampshire	1866	5,260
Rutgers—The State Univ. of New Jersey	1766	19,801
State University of New York (all campuses)	1948	39,635
Pennsylvania State University	1855	21,242
University of Puerto Rico	1903	20,892
University of Rhode Island	1892	6,189
University of Tennessee	1794	13,457
University of Vermont	1791	3,628
West Virginia University	1862	8,282

LAND-GRANT STATE UNIVERSITIES (CONT)

University of Wisconsin	1848	32,835
University of Wyoming	1887	4,988
Total		472,516

SEPARATE LAND-GRANT INSTITUTIONS

Alabama Agricultural and Mechanical College	1875	1,307
Auburn University	1872	9,270
Agricultural Mechanical and Normal College (Arkansas)	1875	1,909
Colorado State University	1870	6,529
Delaware State College	1891	500
Florida Agricultural and Mechanical Univ.	1887	3,480
Fort Valley State College	1895	988
Georgia Institute of Technology	1888	6,754
Purdue University	1874	21,282
Iowa State University of Science and Technology	1858	10,413
Kansas State University	1863	7,850
Kentucky State College	1886	708
Southern University and Agricultural and Mechanical College (Louisiana)	1880	5,827
Maryland State College	1886	545
Michigan State University	1855	26,091
Alcorn Agricultural and Mechanical College	1871	1,183
Mississippi State University	1878	4,876
Lincoln University (Missouri)	1866	1,608
Montana State College	1893	4,289
New Mexico State University	1888	4,565
Agricultural and Technological College of North Carolina	1891	2,534
North Carolina State University of Agriculture and Engineering	1889	7,891
North Dakota State University of Agriculture and Applied Science	1890	3,596
Ohio State University	1870	27,410
Langston University (Oklahoma)	1897	664
Oklahoma State University	1890	11,301
Oregon State University	1868	9,027
South Carolina State College	1896	2,036
Clemson College (South Carolina)	1889	4,102
South Dakota State College	1883	3,127
Tennessee A & I State University	1912	4,000
Agricultural and Mechanical College of Texas	1876	7,719
Arlington State College (Texas)	1895	8,318
Prairie View A & M College (Texas)	1879	3,053
Tarleton State College (Texas)	1899	1,388
Utah State University of Agriculture and Applied Science	1888	7,946
Virginia Polytechnic Institute	1872	7,242
Radford College, Women's Division of V P I	1910	1,672
Virginia State College	1882	3,573
Washington State University	1890	8,243
West Virginia State College	1891	2,153
Massachusetts Institute of Technology (M I T is independent, but has received part of land grant funds from Massachusetts.)	1861	6,454
Cornell University (New York) This independent university is the Land Grant College for New York, under contract with SUNY. The enrollment is included under University total.	1865	11,768
Total		265,191

NORMAL SCHOOLS (OR TEACHERS COLLEGES)
TO STATE COLLEGES AND STATE UNIVERSITIES

Alabama State College	1890	2,444
Florence State College (Alabama)	1872	2,081
Jacksonville State College (Alabama)	1883	2,578
Livingston State College (Alabama)	1840	747
Troy State College (Alabama)	1887	2,073
Arizona State College	1899	2,354
Arizona State University	1885	13,492
Arkansas State Teachers College	1907	2,075
Henderson State Teachers College (Arkansas)	1929	1,590
Alameda State College (California)	1959	1,445
Chico State College (California)	1887	4,044
Fresno State College (California)	1911	7,698
Humboldt State College (California)	1913	2,461
Long Beach State College (California)	1949	11,316
Los Angeles State College (California)	1947	16,592
Orange County State College (California)	1959	1,642
Sacramento State College (California)	1947	7,723
San Diego State College (California)	1897	13,314
San Fernando Valley State College (California)	1958	7,554
San Francisco State College (California)	1899	16,965
San Jose State College (California)	1857	19,168
Sonoma State College (California)	1961	
Stanislaus County State College (California)	1961	
Adams State College of Colorado	1921	1,688
Colorado State College (Greeley, Colorado)	1890	4,570
Western State College of Colorado (Gunnison)	1901	1,667
Central Connecticut State College	1849	3,799
Danbury State College (Connecticut)	1903	1,247
Southern Connecticut State College	1893	3,777
Willimantic State College (Connecticut)	1889	757
District of Columbia Teachers College	1851	1,252
Albany State College (Georgia)	1903	984
Georgia Teachers College	1908	1,764
Valdosta State College (Georgia)	1906	916
Georgia State College for Women	1889	821
Lewis Clark Normal School (Idaho)	1955	319
Illinois State Normal University	1857	5,700
Eastern Illinois University	1895	3,578
Northern Illinois University	1895	8,774
Southern Illinois University	1869	15,223
Western Illinois University	1899	3,617
Ball State Teachers College (Indiana)	1918	8,125
Indiana State College	1865	5,316
State College of Iowa	1876	4,502
Fort Hays Kansas State College	1902	3,191
Kansas State College of Pittsburg	1903	3,420
Kansas State Teachers College	1863	4,878
Eastern Kentucky State College	1906	4,155
Morehead State College (Kentucky)	1922	3,022
Murray State College (Kentucky)	1922	3,674
Western Kentucky State College	1906	5,038
Northwestern State College of Louisiana	1884	3,240
Aroostook State Teachers College (Maine)	1903	244
Farmington State Teachers College (Maine)	1864	534
Fort Kent State Teachers College (Maine)	1878	101
Gorham State Teachers College (Maine)	1878	727

NORMAL SCHOOLS (OR TEACHERS COLLEGES)
TO STATE COLLEGES AND STATE UNIVERSITIES (*Cont*)

Washington State Teachers College (Maine)	1909	328
Coppin State Teachers College (Maryland)	1900	357
State Teachers College (Bowie, Maryland)		355
State Teachers College (Frostburg, Maryland)	1898	1,274
State Teachers College (Salisbury, Maryland)	1925	538
State Teachers College at Towson (Maryland)	1866	1,756
State College (Boston, Massachusetts)	1899	2,779
State College (Bridgewater, Massachusetts)	1840	1,361
State College (Fitchburg, Massachusetts)	1894	1,118
State College (Framingham, Masschusetts)	1839	801
State College (Lowell, Massachusetts)	1894	585
State College (North Adams, Massachusetts)	1894	604
State College (Salem, Massachusetts)	1854	2,292
State College (Westfield, Massachusetts)	1839	1,007
State College (Worcester, Massachusetts)	1871	1,534
Central Michigan University	1892	7,143
Eastern Michigan University	1849	6,939
Northern Michigan College	1899	2,851
Western Michigan University	1903	11,337
Bemidji State College (Minnesota)	1919	1,709
Mankato State College (Minnesota)	1867	6,443
Moorhead State College (Minnesota)	1887	2,112
St. Cloud State College (Minnesota)	1869	4,486
Winona State College (Minnesota)	1858	1,826
Delta State Teachers College (Mississippi)	1924	1,217
Jackson State College (Mississippi)	1877	1,569
Mississippi Southern College	1910	5,261
Central Missouri State College	1871	4,716
Northeast Missouri State College	1867	3,278
Northwest Missouri State College	1905	2,435
Southeast Missouri State College	1873	3,272
Southwest Missouri State College	1906	3,433
Eastern Montana College of Education	1925	1,652
Northern Montana College	1913	707
Western Montana College of Education	1893	587
Nebraska State Teachers College (Chadron)	1911	1,055
Nebraska State Teachers College (Kearney)	1905	2,310
Nebraska State Teachers College (Peru)	1867	789
Wayne Nebraska State Teachers College (Wayne)	1910	1,434
Keene Teachers College (New Hampshire)	1909	1,096
Plymouth Teachers College (New Hampshire)	1871	972
Glassboro State College (New Jersey)	1923	3,312
Jersey City State College (New Jersey)	1929	2,265
Montclair State College (New Jersey)	1908	3,532
Newark State College (New Jersey)	1885	2,639
Paterson State College (New Jersey)	1855	3,281
Trenton State College (New Jersey)	1855	4,103
New Mexico Highlands University	1893	1,265
New Mexico Western College	1893	947
State University College (Albany, New York)	1844	3,546
State University College (Brockport, New York)	1866	2,646
State University College (Buffalo, New York)	1867	4,443
State University College (Cortland, New York)	1866	3,306
State University College (Fredonia, New York)	1886	1,448
State University College (Geneseo, New York)	1867	2,028

NORMAL SCHOOLS (OR TEACHERS COLLEGES)
TO STATE COLLEGES AND STATE UNIVERSITIES *(Cont)*

State University College (New Paltz, New York)	1885	3,025
State University College (Oneonta, New York)	1889	2,681
State University College (Oswego, New York)	1867	3,301
State University College (Plattsburg, New York)	1889	2,077
State University College (Pottsdam, New York)	1866	1,834
Appalachian State Teachers College (North Carolina)	1903	3,093
North Carolina College (Durham)	1910	2,361
East Carolina College	1907	7,113
Elizabeth City State Teachers College (North Carolina)	1891	753
Fayetteville State Teachers College (North Carolina)	1867	863
Western Carolina College (North Carolina)	1889	2,093
Winston-Salem Teachers College (North Carolina)	1892	1,078
Dickinson State Teachers College (North Dakota)	1920	820
Ellendale State Teachers College (North Dakota)	1889	196
Mayville State Teachers College (North Dakota)	1890	622
Minot State Teachers College (North Dakota)	1913	1,641
Valley City State Teachers College (North Dakota)	1890	830
Bowling Green State University (Ohio)	1910	7,657
Central State College (Ohio)	1887	2,029
Kent State University (Ohio)	1910	13,150
Central State College (Oklahoma)	1890	4,622
East Central State College (Oklahoma)	1909	1,881
Northeastern State College (Oklahoma)	1846	3,167
Northwestern State College (Oklahoma)	1897	1,320
Southeastern State College (Oklahoma)	1909	1,924
Southwestern State College (Oklahoma)	1901	2,355
Eastern Oregon College	1929	1,068
Oregon College of Education	1882	1,285
Portland State College (Oregon)	1955	5,268
Southern Oregon College	1926	1,621
Bloomsburg State College (Pennsylvania)	1839	1,978
California State College (Pennsylvania)	1852	2,923
Cheyney State College (Pennsylvania)	1837	896
Clairon State College (Pennsylvania)	1867	1,810
East Stroudsburg State College (Pennsylvania)	1893	1,606
Edinboro State College (Pennsylvania)	1857	1,899
Indiana State College (Pennsylvania)	1875	4,080
Kutztown State College (Pennsylvania)	1860	1,958
Lock Haven State College (Pennsylvania)	1870	1,266
Mansfield State College (Pennsylvania)	1857	1,155
Millersville State College (Pennsylvania)	1855	2,058
Shippensburg State College (Pennsylvania)	1871	1,564
Slippery Rock State College (Pennsylvania)	1889	1,606
West Chester State College (Pennsylvania)	1871	3,002
Rhode Island College	1854	2,572
Black Hills Teachers College (South Dakota)	1883	1,040
Gen. Beadle State Teachers College (South Dakota)	1881	478
Northern State Teachers College (South Dakota)	1901	1,645
Southern State Teachers College (South Dakota)	1881	682
Austin Peay State College (Tennessee)	1929	1,979
East Tennessee State College (Tennessee)	1911	4,915
Memphis State University (Tennessee)	1912	6,527
Middle Tennessee State College (Tennessee)	1911	3,358
East Texas State College	1889	3,519
North Texas State University	1890	8,835

NORMAL SCHOOLS (OR TEACHERS COLLEGES)
TO STATE COLLEGES AND STATE UNIVERSITIES (CONT)

Sam Houston State Teachers College (Texas)	1879	5,017
Southwest Texas State College	1898	2,869
Stephen F. Austin State College (Texas)	1923	2,387
Sul Ross State College (Texas)	1917	1,260
West Texas State College	1910	3,462
Castleton Teachers College (Vermont)	1867	473
Johnson Teachers College (Vermont)	1867	215
Lyndon Teachers College (Vermont)	1911	279
Longwood College (Virginia)	1884	1,173
Madison College (Virginia)	1908	1,674
Central Washington State College	1890	2,873
Eastern Washington State College	1890	2,873
Western Washington State College	1899	3,824
Bluefield State College (West Virginia)	1895	580
Concord College (West Virginia)	1875	1,168
Fairmont State College (West Virginia)	1867	1,488
Glenville State College (West Virginia)	1872	854
Marshall University (West Virginia)	1837	4,750
Shepherd State College (West Virginia)	1871	933
West Liberty State College (West Virginia)	1837	1,628
Stout State College (Wisconsin)	1893	1,652
Wisconsin State College (Eau Claire)	1916	2,609
Wisconsin State College (La Crosse)	1909	2,042
Wisconsin State College (Oshkosh)	1871	3,957
Wisconsin State College (River Falls)	1874	1,911
Wisconsin State College (Stevens Point)	1894	2,823
Wisconsin State College (Superior)	1896	1,572
Wisconsin State College (Whitewater)	1868	3,082
Wisconsin State College and Institute of Technology	1866	2,307
	Total	592,869

STATE JUNIOR COLLEGES

Anchorage Community College (Alaska)	1953	1,205
Juneau-Douglas Community College (Alaska)	1956	326
Ketchikan Community College (Alaska)	1954	189
Palmer Community College (Alaska)	1958	70
Fort Lewis A & M College (Colorado)	1911	749
Abraham Baldwin Agricultural College (Georgia)	1933	702
Armstrong College of Savannah (Georgia)	1935	985
Augusta College (Georgia)	1925	992
Columbus College (Georgia)	1958	659
Georgia Southwestern College	1908	484
Middle Georgia College	1928	600
South Georgia College	1906	641
St. Mary's Seminary Junior College (Maryland)	1839	258
New Hampshire Technical Institute (Manchester)	1946	228
New Hampshire Technical Institute (Portsmouth)	1945	135
Trenton Junior College (New Jersey)	1947	1,040
New Mexico Military Institute	1891	319
State University Agricultural & Technical Institute (Alfred, New York)	1908	1,473
State University Agricultural & Technical Institute (Canton, New York)	1907	675
State University Agricultural & Technical Institute (Cobleskill, New York)	1911	654

STATE JUNIOR COLLEGES

State University Agricultural & Technical Institute (Delhi, New York)	1913	521
State University Agricultural & Technical Institute (Farmingdale, New York)	1912	1,729
State University Agricultural & Technical Institute (Morrisville, New York)	1910	835
North Dakota School of Forestry	1906	220
North Dakota State School of Science	1903	348
Cameron State A & M College (Oklahoma)	1908	1,542
Connors State Agricultural College (Oklahoma)	1909	472
Eastern Oklahoma A & M College (Oklahoma)	1909	713
Murray State Agricultural College (Oklahoma)	1908	404
Northeastern Oklahoma A & M College	1919	1,243
Northern Oklahoma Junior College	1901	589
Oklahoma Military College	1919	217
Oregon Technical Institute	1947	902
Dixie Junior College (Utah)	1916	347
Weber College (Utah)	1889	2,878
Potomac State College of West Virginia University	1901	654
	Total	25,998

FORMER JUNIOR COLLEGES

West Georgia College (Carrollton)	1933	1,089
McNeese State College (Louisiana)	1939	2,772
Northeast Louisiana State College	1931	2,992
Southeastern Louisiana College	1925	2,577
Eastern New Mexico University	1934	2,673
Midwestern University (Texas)	1922	1,924
Texas Southern University	1947	3,600
Northern Virginia Center	1948	2,500
	Total	20,127

SINGLE-PURPOSE INSTITUTIONS

California Maritime Academy	1929	259
Colorado School of Mines	1874	1,037
Georgia State College	1914	3,447
Medical College of Georgia	1828	470
Maine Maritime Academy	1941	350
Massachusetts College of Art	1873	509
Massachusetts Maritime Academy	1891	198
Michigan College of Mining and Technology	1885	3,289
Missouri School of Mines and Metallurgy	1870	3,315
Montana School of Mines	1893	380
New Mexico Institution of Mining and Technology	1889	258
The Citadel (South Carolina)	1842	1,966
Medical College of South Carolina	1823	642
South Dakota School of Mines and Technology	1885	985
Texas College of Arts and Industries	1925	3,292
Medical College of Virginia	1838	1,124
Virginia Military Institute	1839	1,073
	Total	22,594

WOMEN'S COLLEGES

Mississippi State College for Women	1884	1,730
Womens College of University of North Carolina	1891	3,139
Oklahoma College for Women	1908	652
Winthrop College (South Carolina)	1886	1,993
Texas Woman's University	1901	2,766
	Total	10,280

FORMER WOMEN'S COLLEGES

Alabama College	1896	1,394
Florida State University	1857	9,835
	Total	11,229

NON-LAND-GRANT TECHNICAL COLLEGES

Arkansas Polytechnic College	1909	1,434
Arkansas State College	1909	3,685
Arkansas Agricultural and Mechanical College	1909	1,035
Southern State College (Arkansas)	1909	1,262
California State Polytechnic College	1901	7,850
North Georgia College	1873	927
Savannah State College	1891	1,065
Grambling College (Louisiana)	1901	2,758
Idaho State College	1901	2,532
Louisiana Polytechnic Institute	1894	3,947
University of Southwestern Louisiana	1898	5,421
Bradford Durfee College of Technology (Massachusetts)	1899	602
Lowell Technological Institute (Massachusetts)	1895	1,318
New Bedford Institute of Technology (Massachusetts)	1895	589
Ferris Institute (Michigan)	1884	3,013
Mississippi Vocational College	1949	910
Newark College of Engineering (New Jersey)	1881	3,824
Panhandle Agricultural and Mechanical College (Oklahoma)	1909	1,024
Tennessee Polytechnic Institute	1915	3,119
Lamar State College of Technology (Texas)	1923	5,379
Texas Technological College	1923	10,212
West Virginia Institute of Technology	1895	995
	Total	62,901

OTHER STATE COLLEGES AND UNIVERSITIES

University of South Florida	1956	2,982
Francis T. Nicholls State College (Louisiana)	1948	1,184
Morgan State College (Maryland)	1867	2,589
Wayne State University (Michigan)	1868	20,605
Pembroke State College (North Carolina)	1887	570
Texas Western College	1913	4,833
College of William and Mary (Virginia)	1693	8,638
	Total	41,401

Index